ARTISANAL SOAPS

MAKE YOUR OWN CUSTOM, HANDCRAFTED SOAPS!

 ALICIA GROSSO

FALL RIVER PRESS

New York

FALL RIVER PRESS

New York

An Imprint of Sterling Publishing Co., Inc.
1166 Avenue of the Americas
New York, NY 10036

ISBN 978-1-4351-6701-8

For information about custom editions, special sales, and premium and corporate purchases, please
contact Sterling Special Sales at 800-805-5489 or specialsales@sterlingpublishing.com.

Manufactured in China

2 4 6 8 10 9 7 5 3 1

sterlingpublishing.com

Cover design by Stephanie Hannus

Image credits:
Cover photography by Stephanie Hannus
Shutterstock: ©Accesslab 122; ©Elena Elisseeva 194; ©Marc_Espolet 16, 202; ©Shawn Hempel 70;
©Anna Hoychuk 25; ©Nadisja 124; ©Sirirath Panitchayarom 121; ©Uximetc Pavel 188; ©Hank Shiffman 54;
DepositPhotos: ©Mihai Simonia 154;
iStock: 26; ©Chris Gramly 4; ©Paul Grecaud 8; ©Meral Yildirim 38; ©Valentyn Volkov 56;
©Grafvision 59; ©Chamille White 96; ©Irina Burakova 172; ©inspired_by_the_light 198

CONTENTS

INTRODUCTION

Soaps filled with basil, lavender, or lemon verbena that you've grown in your garden. Soaps scented with essential oils such as oakmoss, rose, or tea tree, picked up at your local market. Soaps striped in scarlet, indigo, and gold that bring the vibrant colors of the farmers' market into your home.

DIY Artisanal Soaps will teach you everything you need to know to join the community of soapmakers across the country. In doing so, you'll find that this simple household substance will gain a completely new meaning for you. Your soaps will be filled with ingredients you've found or purchased at local markets and stands, ranging from beeswax to bacon, mango butter to soy oil. You'll find yourself searching through your pantry, garden, and local farm produce stands for plants, oils, and fruits you can put into your soaps. You'll search for molds and tools to shape your bars in countless creative ways. And you'll learn how to make bar and liquid soaps, cold- and hot-process soaps, and hand-milled soaps safely and easily in the comfort of your own kitchen.

Homemade soap has these benefits:

It's natural. Homemade artisan soap isn't something that's churned out of a factory, chock-full of potentially harmful chemicals. You make it with natural ingredients that you've chosen. After all, you know what's best for you and your family. You can avoid anything to which you're allergic and focus on those substances you enjoy most.

It's creative. Making soap means more than just following a series of steps in a recipe book. It's finding new ways of creating something that smells great and looks inviting. Soapmaking, as many have found, is a way to express yourself as you dream up new recipes and mold the soap into innovative forms.

It's energizing. Handmade soap makes you feel good because it reminds you that you made it. As you soak in a bath or stand in the shower, you'll enjoy using something that's the product of your vision and creativity. You'll enjoy combining different ingredients in your soaps, experimenting with fragrances, colors, and textures until you discover just the right one for you.

Soapmaking is a way of using natural ingredients to create an item that you both love and love to use. In fact, you'll soon find that you love this creative process so much that you'll want to share your artisanal soaps with others, which is why you'll find suggestions throughout the book on how to lovingly prepare your products for gifting, sharing, and selling. So start experiencing the home-grown pleasures of soapmaking, and bring the scents of farm and garden into your own home.

SAFETY NOTE

Soapmaking at home can be hazardous. Heat and caustics are the primary potential dangers. If you fear that you cannot sufficiently control your surroundings to keep and use soapmaking materials safely, do not make soap at home. However, soap is made without accident every day by thousands of home soapmakers. The basic safety gear you'll need is eye protection, gloves, protective mitts, a painter's paper dust mask or filter mask, a fire extinguisher, and vinegar.

EYE PROTECTION

Internet soapmaking-supply houses and hardware stores stock a variety of eye protection products. Make sure that the eye protection you use is resistant to impact, caustics, and heat. If you wear glasses, get goggles that are large enough to wear over them. Be particular as you shop for eye protection. Never take chances with the health and safety of your eyes.

The danger to your eyes comes from the potential of lye particles, lye solution, raw soap, hot oils, and other liquids splashing you in the face. In methods that do not use caustics to create soap, the potential hazards are hot melted soap and steam. As long as you work mindfully, you will experience very few—if any—splashing events. However, you do not want to be caught unprotected if one should occur.

At the very least, caustics will cause surface irritation to the skin on your face. At the worst, you can be blinded if you splash lye solution in your eyes. Be sure to have an emergency plan just in case an accident should happen.

GLOVES AND/OR PROTECTIVE MITTS

Regular rubber kitchen gloves provide appropriate protection for your hands and lower arms. Make sure the gloves you buy have textured fingers so that you can keep a firm grip on your equipment. Some soapmakers prefer heavy-duty gloves. Just be sure you can use your fingers freely.

Thin "examination" gloves are sufficient for handling partly cured soap. You can find these in the pharmacy section of a mass-market store and at drugstores. If you are sensitive to latex, you can buy gloves made from thin vinyl. Check your gloves regularly for holes and splits. Replace them before you need to.

When you are finished with your soapmaking project for the day, clean your gloves well with soap and water. If you clean them and dry them, they'll last quite some time. Turn them inside-out to dry and store them only after they're completely dry.

Be sure to protect your arms above the gloves with a long-sleeved shirt. An oversized button-up shirt with sleeves you can roll up is ideal.

Remember that you're not going to go around carelessly splashing lye. You will have everything prepared so you won't be running here and there, dripping caustics and hot soap around. Just use common sense and be sure you protect yourself and household surfaces.

You should also have some heavy-duty oven mitts handy for lifting hot containers from the stove or other surfaces. Be sure to clean them regularly, since they can quickly build up soap components.

PAINTER'S PAPER DUST MASK OR FILTER MASK

If you're making soap with lye, it can cause dangerous fumes. Usually it is enough just to stand back and not breathe the fumes, but if you are concerned about sensitivity to them, wear a painter's paper dust mask or filter mask over your mouth and nose.

FIRE EXTINGUISHER

Whenever you are working with a stove, hotplate, or other heat source, you need to have a fire extinguisher within easy reach. Make sure your fire extinguisher is charged and ready to go. The time you need the fire extinguisher is not the time to wonder where it is or if it's charged. Read the instructions so that you know how to use it. Also be sure to review basic kitchen safety procedures. For example, you would never throw water on an oil fire, and you would always use protective mitts when handling hot pans and utensils.

VINEGAR

Keep a gallon jug of white vinegar handy and put some in a labeled spray bottle. White vinegar is a weak acid that neutralizes the caustic base of the lye. If you come in contact with lye or raw soap batter, rinse your skin with water first, then douse the area with vinegar. Then rinse again with water and finally wash with soap and water. Don't wait to finish stirring your batch before rinsing and neutralizing a smear of raw soap from your skin. Do it as soon as it gets on you.

PHYSICIAN'S CONTACT INFORMATION

Finally, take note that it's always a good idea to post the phone numbers of your physician, emergency room, and poison control center where they are easily seen. If you were to have an accident, you would be able to get the help you need more quickly.

None of the previous should scare you away from soapmaking. After all, thousands of people make soap every day. However, it's always of primary importance to put safety first and fun second. Once you have the safety measures in place, you can relax and enjoy the fun of soapmaking!

CHAPTER ONE

WHAT YOU'LL NEED

In addition to the safety equipment we talked about in the previous section, there are some basic tools and utensils you'll need for soapmaking. Note that these are just the beginning. As you increase your soapmaking skills, you'll find other pieces of equipment come in handy; some you'll even start to regard as essential. But here are the basics.

POTS AND PANS

When buying your soapmaking pots and pans, stainless steel is the way to go. You can find stainless steel pots and pans at extremely reasonable prices at restaurant supply, warehouse, discount, and thrift stores.

Why stainless steel? Because you absolutely must not use nonstick, aluminum, cast iron, or tin. These materials are called reactive because they will react with the soaps, ruining both soap and pan. Do not even try "just to see." They will react badly, even violently and toxically, with the lye used in the soapmaking process.

What about enameled pans? It's true that many soapmakers use enameled pots with no trouble at all, but you must check them for pits and chips that will expose your soap to the reactive metal underneath.

Stock Pot

Stainless steel stock pots are perfect for the 4- and 8-pound cold-process recipes in this book. An 8-quart will hold 4-pound recipes, and a 12-quart stock pot will hold 8-pound recipes, with room to stir. It is helpful if the stock pots have gradient marks that indicate the volume, although it isn't necessary.

Double Boiler

Double boilers are used in many kinds of soapmaking. The basic 2-quart, two-part stainless-steel double boiler is perfect for the soap-casting recipes in this book. You can improvise a double boiler using a saucepan and a stainless steel mixing bowl that rests securely but not tightly on the pan. (When using any kind of double boiler always be sure not to let it boil dry.)

GET A THERMOMETER

Along with all the pots and pans, you will need an instant-read thermometer. There are many instances in soapmaking where accurate measure of temperature is essential. Get two, as you may need to measure the temperatures of two containers at the same time.

Slow Cooker

All the hot-process and hand-milling recipes in this book call for the use of a slow cooker. You'll need a 3½-quart slow cooker with a removable crock portion and heat settings of high and low. Although it would probably be safe, don't use a slow cooker for food once it's been used for soaping.

It is essential in hot-process recipes that the slow cooker be just the right size for the batch you are making. If it's too small or too large, the soap won't process properly. It can overheat, overflow, or otherwise not work. Check the recipe for size requirements.

UTENSILS

There are many types of utensils to choose from in soapmaking: stainless steel, silicone, and wooden.

Stainless Steel Utensils

Stainless steel stirring spoons, slotted spoons, potato mashers, and ladles are all very useful. You probably already have these in your kitchen, and it is safe to use them for your first few batches. As long as you clean them thoroughly, there is no danger in using them for food afterward because the metal does not readily absorb or react with the soap.

If you find yourself making a great deal of soap, invest the time and money in stainless steel tools just for soaping. Mass-market, thrift, and restaurant supply stores sell many grades of tools. While you don't need the super-fancy "chef's choice" utensils, choose products that offer sound construction and ease of handling. Keep in mind that you'll need at least one spoon with which to stir the lye. Metal spoons are generally better for this than plastic ones.

Silicone Utensils

Silicone rubber scrapers, or what many people call "spatulas," are indispensable tools. Choose a one-piece model so you will never lose the scraper part in a batch of soap. You don't want to stick your gloved fingers into a batch of raw soap, fishing around for a slippery piece of rubber.

Wooden Utensils

There is a certain romance to stirring your soap with a wooden spoon. It feels more "primitive," the kind of thing our pioneer ancestors used to do. If you want to do this, you need to be sure the spoon is splinter-free and sturdy enough to stir thickening soap batter. In making lye-based soaps, the lye will eventually "eat" the wood, rendering it useless.

HOW ARE YOUR STAINLESS STEEL TOOLS CONSTRUCTED?

Some stainless steel tools are held together with reactive metal screws, bolts, or brads. You probably won't be able to tell what type of metal the fasteners are, so choose utensils that are all one piece or have "all stainless construction" printed on the package. If you're in doubt, pass it by.

You can purchase beautifully crafted hardwood soap-stirring spoons, and although you can certainly use them to stir soap, they are, perhaps, best displayed in your soapmaking area. Many soapers like the feel of getting the saponification process going with wood. Then they switch to silicone scrapers, whisks, hand blenders, or a combination of these.

> **ONLY FOR SOAP**
>
> *If you decide to add wooden utensils to your collection, be sure that you never use wooden spoons for food once they've been used for soap. The wood absorbs the caustics and finished soap.*

You will also find chopsticks, bamboo skewers, and plastic picnic-type utensils very useful. Be sure to clean them well after using and never use them for food after using them for soap. Discard wooden utensils when they show signs of wear. You don't want the splintered remains of a bamboo skewer or a random picnic fork tine showing up in a bar of soap.

MEASURING EQUIPMENT

Don't spend a fortune on fancy measuring cups and spoons from gourmet shops; inexpensive measuring tools will do just fine. Heat-safe glass measuring cups in a variety of sizes are nearly as indispensable as your stainless steel pans. Heavy-duty glass measures with graded measurements on the sides are available at grocery, mass-market, and drug stores. It is tempting to use the attractive thinner heatproof glass, but just stick to the heavy-duty variety as the thin glass will shatter.

The small-batch cold-process recipes in this book call for two 4-cup measures: one for mixing the lye solution and the other for mixing the oils and stirring the soap. The measures are also used in some liquid, melt-and-pour, and hand-milling techniques. They are, of course, always useful for measuring water.

Sets of stainless steel measuring cups and spoons are used in nearly all techniques. It's best to steer clear of plastic measuring cups and spoons. While they can be good for some things, they may be corroded by essential oils and fragrance oils, or marred by heat.

HAND BLENDER

The hand blender, or immersion blender, is a blessing to soapmakers who make soap with lye. The blender shortens the stirring time to minutes rather than hours. There are many varieties of hand blenders, ranging in price from less than $10 to more than $100. Look for an inexpensive blender that has an all-plastic housing, stainless steel blade, and two speeds.

The hand blender you choose for making soap needs to have a shaft long enough to reach to the bottom of your soap pan without being immersed above the immersion limit line. If you immerse your hand blender too deeply, you will ruin the motor. Keep this in mind when you're cleaning it, too.

Using a hand blender can speed up the soaping process, but you need to use it correctly. Hand-stir a number of batches before you use the hand blender so you have a slow, close-up look at the saponification process. Hand-blending speeds up the process so much that you may find yourself with a heavily traced batch before you've made any additions.

Here are a few blending tips:

- When you immerse the blender in the oils and lye mixture, tip it to the side to release the air bubble beneath it. You don't want to incorporate air into your soap.

- Make sure the hand blender is near the bottom of the mixing pan before you turn it on.

- Use the low speed in short bursts to get an idea of how fast the batch is going to trace.

- If you are making a number of batches in a row, you don't need to completely clean the hand blender. Unplug it and wipe it well. The tiny amount of soap clinging to the hand blender will help start the saponification of the next batch.

- Use your spatula to continually scrape the sides of the pan as you blend, keeping the entire mass in motion. You can use the stick of the blender to move the mass around in the pan when you've let up on the power button.

- Be sure the blade has stopped moving before you take the blender out of the pan so that you don't splatter raw soap.

- When you are done for the day, unplug the hand blender and clean it well. As with other electric appliances, don't immerse it in water. Wipe it down to remove most of the soap residue. Then use a soapy sponge to clean it without immersing it.

SOAP MOLDS

Not very many years ago, the variety of soap molds was pretty dismal. Soapmakers made do with molds intended for gelatin desserts and candles. They improvised with cardboard boxes, plastic storage ware, and ice-cube trays.

Today there is an inspiring array of molds created just for soapmaking! From a clever and simple slab mold to the most delicate fancy design, the variety and quality has increased exponentially.

Creating Your Own Molds

Your first batches of soap will very probably be poured into "found" molds. Shoeboxes lined with plastic bags, baby-wipe containers, inexpensive plastic storage containers, and more have all been pressed into service as soap molds. You can use tubes from paper towels or toilet paper rolls. Empty plastic wrap and aluminum foil boxes make small, lidded molds. Artisan soapmakers do not need the latest advance in soap-mold technology. Your mold needs and desires will grow as you gain experience, and you'll find more objects you can use as molds. (For further discussion of making your own molds, see Appendix B.)

If you're using something plastic for a mold, such as a baby-wipe container, be sure to test it for heat resistance. Because of the high temperatures involved in soapmaking, you need plastics that will not collapse when exposed to hot soap. The easiest way to check a mold for heat safety is to place it in the sink and fill it with boiling water. If it melts, it is obviously not going to be useful. If it warps and distorts, it is not a good choice either.

MAKING A PLASTIC-LINED MOLD

You can make a basic mold from a cardboard box lined with a plastic garbage bag. To be sure the box will hold the soap batch, measure an equivalent amount of water and pour it into the lined mold. If it doesn't fit, keep testing until you get just the size box you want.

Removing Soap from Molds

You may need some additional supplies to make it easier to get your soap out of its mold. Soapmakers struggle with unmolding all the time. A simple way to ensure ease of release is to line the bottom and sides of the mold. You can brush vegetable oil lightly on the inside of the mold. Then cut plastic sheeting, freezer paper, overhead projector transparency, or other similar materials to size and press onto the oiled surface. Smooth out bumps and creases in the liner to ensure smooth surfaces on your soap. When the soap is ready to unmold, if all has gone as it should, all you'll have to do is turn the mold over, and the beautiful soap will just plop out onto the table. Remove the liner and clean it up for reuse.

MY SOAP WON'T COME OUT OF THE MOLD

If after a few days the soap won't release from the mold, put it in the freezer for half an hour and try again. If you've repeatedly frozen the soap and it still won't come out, just pry it out and form it into a soap ball. Remember, if something doesn't work, relax. You can always try again!

Making Polymer Clay Molds

You can make your own small molds for casting soap using flexible polymer clay. This type of mold-making is best suited for small soaps to either use as-is or as embeds. You make an impression of an object you'd like to replicate as a soap, bake the clay, then use the still-flexible form as a mold. It will become brittle over time, but it is a wonderful way to make something utterly, uniquely yours.

There is a kind of polymer clay that is specifically made to be used in mold-making, so be sure to get the right thing. "Regular" polymer clay bakes hard and will not flex.

Choose a small object that is wider at the bottom than it is at the top so that the hardened soap will come out easily. You can achieve quite a lot of detail with this medium, so it works beautifully with shells, pendants, small statues, and even rubber stamps.

Follow these simple instructions:

- Work the flexible polymer clay with your hands to make it pliable.

- Make a tablet shape—flat on the bottom and on the top with a large enough surface area for the design, and deep enough to take the full impression.

- Lightly spritz the surface of the object with water and wipe off drips. The fine coating of water will help release the object from the clay.

- Push the object into the clay, narrow end first, and remove it quickly. If the impression is good, use it. If the impression is unclear, re-form the tablet and try again.

- Bake the flexible mold clay as directed on the package. Generally, the temperature is 275°F and the time is 10 minutes per ¼" of thickness.

- When the clay is baked, remove it to a heatproof surface to cool.

Keep in mind that the clay will get softer and warmer the more you work it with your hands, so let it cool between shapings for better results. You can use one tablet for a few small impressions. When using multiple items on one tablet, be sure to allow room for the clay to move and spread between images without distortion.

You can use your new mold as soon as it is cool. Be sure to store it in a dry place where it won't be exposed to light or heat. It will decay over time, but with gentle use you should be able to use it over and over.

CUTTING TOOLS

The simplest soap cutter is a stainless steel table knife. Most soapers prefer nonserrated knives since they make a clean cut.

Artisan soapmakers have adapted all kinds of tools into soap cutters. Dough scrapers borrowed from baking and putty knives and drywall tape spreaders borrowed from home improvement work very well. Even a wire cheese cutter can be put to good use for smaller bars.

Plans for a simple set of cutters for bigger blocks of soap are in Appendix B.

CHAPTER TWO

HOW TO GET STARTED

All right. You've assembled your equipment (including your all-important safety equipment), and you're ready to make your first bar of soap.

Now what?

Any discussion of soap begins with lye. If you've read anything about soapmaking or seen videos about it on YouTube, you probably know this already, but it's time to take a closer look at lye and the role it plays in soap.

The transformation of oils into soap, called saponification, can only happen through the interaction of a lye solution with oils. Be careful, though! Used carelessly, lye can cause severe burns and serious injury. Even when extreme care is taken, there is a potential for injury. I can't overemphasize the necessity of smart safety practices when handling lye, lye solutions, raw, and "young" soap. In this chapter you'll learn how to make lye soap safely at home.

WHAT IS LYE?

Lye is a caustic that is an ingredient of all soap. Home soapmakers use two kinds of lye: sodium hydroxide, which is used to make solid soap, and potassium hydroxide, which is used to make liquid soap. In this section you will learn about each.

Sodium Hydroxide

Sodium hydroxide (chemical formula NaOH) is what most people mean when they say "lye." Sodium hydroxide is easily available in 18-ounce plastic cans at grocery, hardware, and restaurant supply stores. It is generally stocked alongside the drain cleaners. Don't buy anything other than pure sodium hydroxide. There are other drain cleaners available, but they include substances that are not at all suitable for soapmaking. You may also purchase sodium hydroxide from soapmaking suppliers. It is considered a hazardous material, and there are restrictions to the amount you can order through the mail. Check with the supplier for the regulations in your area. If you plan to make a great deal of soap, it's a good idea to find a local supplier where you can buy lye in bulk.

Because it is an ingredient in the manufacture of the dangerous, illegal drug methamphetamine, also known as "meth" or "crank," sodium hydroxide is controlled in some states. People who manufacture large amounts of soap, and therefore need to keep large amounts of lye on hand, must register it with local agencies.

Store your sodium hydroxide in a safe, dry place. The space under the kitchen sink is not a good idea, especially if you have kids. Many home soapers have a "lye safe" just for lye storage. Lye safes can range from a box in the garage clearly marked "Lye! Do Not Touch!" to a metal cabinet with locking doors.

KEEP AWAY FROM CHILDREN AND PETS

The safety of children and pets is a primary concern. If you live with an adult with special needs, you must also take that situation into consideration. Educate them not to touch the lye safe and to stay away from cooling lye solutions while you are making soap.

You can make a practical and easy-to-create lye safe from a plastic storage box with a tightly fitting lid. Label it clearly and store it where you think is safest in your home. Storing your lye safe on a high shelf isn't necessarily recommended, since you can easily drop it, especially if you keep more than a few pounds. Keeping it on the floor of a closet can work, as can the floor of the garage. If you find yourself worrying about the safe storage of your soapmaking caustics, perhaps you should employ one or more of the techniques that do not use lye. Pay attention to your intuition.

In your lye safe, keep the plastic cans of lye in plastic bags. Label three bags: one for unopened cans, one for partially used cans, and one for empties. Take care how you dispose of empty containers. Neutralize the lye dust by rinsing the containers with a vinegar-and-water solution. If you have a hazardous material drop-off day in your community, take your empty lye cans to the collection point.

Potassium Hydroxide

Potassium hydroxide (chemical formula KOH) is a type of caustic used to make liquid soap. It is important to note that potassium hydroxide and sodium hydroxide are *not* interchangeable in soap recipes. Different amounts of each are needed to saponify the same amount of fats. If you make both liquid and solid soaps, be sure to keep your instructions and saponification charts for each clearly marked.

Potassium hydroxide is more difficult to find than sodium hydroxide. You can order it from soap supply houses and buy it at chemical supply stores. As usual with soapmaking, the Internet is your best resource.

Store potassium hydroxide as you would sodium hydroxide: in a safe spot and clearly labeled.

MAKING SOAP WITH LYE

In the simplest terms, you combine lye, oils, and a liquid to make soap. The liquid may be water, milk, herbal infusions, or any liquid with a relatively neutral pH. Each liquid requires specific soapmaking techniques.

The purpose of liquid in lye soapmaking is to get the lye and the oils together. In a solution with water, lye molecules are more easily able to reach the molecules of oil. When they come in contact, the lye and oil molecules all rearrange themselves and become soap and glycerin. If you were to simply add lye to oil, without the liquid, the transformation process would be different, and you'd end up with a big, caustic mess.

In this book, the amount of lye used in a recipe depends on how much of each oil you use. Each oil has a saponification value. This is the amount of lye it takes to turn 1 ounce of oil into soap. Soap recipes are calculated to make sure they have the proper balance of oils, water, and lye.

Combining Lye with Water

An important step in soapmaking is combining lye with water. This creates an extremely violent, volatile chemical reaction. *It is essential that you add the lye to the water rather than the water to the lye.* When you add water to lye, the chemical reaction causes the water and lye solution to heat almost immediately to nearly boiling. If water is poured onto the lye, it forms a crust over the top of the lye, which seals in the reaction below. The reaction of the lye and water proceeds normally but in a confined space, causing a buildup of heat energy that eventually bursts open like a bomb, showering the area with dangerously caustic material.

ADD LYE TO COLD WATER

Always add lye to cold liquid. The reaction is so violent and rapid that if you add lye to hot liquid, you'll be dangerously close to or over the boiling point in no time. Never add lye to hot liquid.

But even when you correctly add lye to cold water, do so with care. When you add the lye to the liquid, the solution will heat up very fast and will steam. Do not breathe the fumes. As stated earlier, usually it is enough just to stand back and not breathe the fumes, but if you are concerned about sensitivity to lye fumes, wear a painter's paper dust mask or filter mask over your mouth and nose. If you are very sensitive to chemicals, lye soapmaking may not be for you. Consider one of the methods of making soap at home in which you don't have to use lye.

Lye Solution Temperature

The lye-and-water solution will heat up to about 180°F. You need to let the solution cool before combining it with the prepared oils. Soapmaking temperatures can range from room temperature (as long as the room is warm enough to keep the oils liquid) to as high as 120°F.

You can take the steaming lye solution outside to let it cool. Just be sure it is in a safe place where no one can get to it and it won't get knocked over. It is also a good idea to cover the container so no leaves or other debris fall into it.

Some soapmakers insist that the temperatures of the lye solution and the oil combination must be exactly the same. Others never even check the temperature. You should start learning your soapmaking techniques by following the temperature guides given in the recipe you are using. After a lot of experience with variations in temperatures, and how those variations affect the process and the product, you can then make your own decisions about how to manage temperature.

CHOOSING A LIQUID

Water is the most commonly used liquid in soapmaking. You can make perfectly usable soap with tap water, but I suggest that you use purified water. You can use water that has been filtered by an on-the-tap filter or a pour-through filter, which will remove some of the undesirable material from your water. Or you can purchase distilled or purified or drinking water at the grocery store. Distilled is preferred by many artisan soapmakers since we want our soap to be natural and pure, and distilled water is as pure as you can get. Try a few different kinds to see which one you like. You may even find you don't notice a difference at all, so you can save some money using tap water.

Different Types of Water

Another type of water you can use is seawater, which adds natural salt and other minerals to your soap. Don't collect your seawater in a polluted area, or you'll be adding all kinds of things to your soaps that you don't want. Since seawater contains plant life, it is a good idea to use it right away because the microorganisms will die and decay and make the water unsuitable to use.

SOAPS AS SOUVENIRS

Soapmaking can help you create a lasting souvenir of a vacation or pilgrimage. At the ocean, collect some water and some sand in an empty plastic drink bottle. You can make a 1-pound soap batch using just 6 ounces of water. At the family cabin on the lake, collect some lake water and dry some plant matter from the lakeside. Every time you lather up you'll have the satisfaction of thinking about your vacation with nature.

Throughout history, people have venerated wells by dedicating them to goddesses, saints, and other religious figures. Waters from some wells are thought to have healing properties. Make soap from the well water, perhaps leaving it unscented and uncolored to focus on the water itself, or add botanicals, sand, and even soil from the site as well. Be respectful, of course, and don't strip the area of flowers and stones.

If you live in an unpolluted area, you can use collected rainwater in soapmaking. Many soapers find that rainwater is soft and useful for soapmaking. If you leave out containers to collect rainwater, tip them over during mosquito egg-laying season, or you will find yourself with a homegrown herd of buzzing biters.

Scented waters—such as those often used in cooking—make excellent liquids for soapmaking. Rosewater and orange flower water can be found in the Middle Eastern food sections of large groceries and at specialty food stores. They are used to flavor sweets in cooking, and they retain a certain amount of their fragrance in soapmaking.

Making Soap with Milk

Milk soaps have been used for years for their skin-softening properties. The combination of butterfat and lactic acid makes for a very skin-smoothing soap. There are some special requirements to using milk as your liquid. Follow some simple procedures, and you'll be very happy with your milk soaps.

Cow's milk makes excellent soap. Determine the butterfat percentage you want depending on the result you want. If you want the exfoliating properties of lactic acid without the moisturizing properties of butterfat, use nonfat milk. At the other extreme, use half-and-half or even cream for extremely creamy, rich soap. Other milk products that are popular with soapmakers are buttermilk, evaporated milk (not condensed milk!), powdered milk, and coconut milk (although it's not really "milk").

Controlling the Temperature

The main thing about making soap with milk is that you must control the temperature of the milk-lye solution. The solution to the potential problem is simple: freeze the milk! Weigh the amount of milk you want to use and place it in a freezer-safe container. The wider and shallower the container is, the faster it will freeze. When the milk is nearly solid, take it out of the freezer and stir. It is ready to use if it is firmly slushy.

GOAT'S MILK SOAP

Goat's milk soap is extremely popular for use in artisan soapmaking. If you live in a rural area and are so inclined you may even keep goats yourself. If you do this, or know someone who does, get some milk and make soap!

Adding the Lye

Place the slushy milk in a large heatproof glass or stainless steel bowl. The bowl needs to be big enough to hold the milk when it thaws, plus the volume of the lye. There should also be some headroom to contain sloshing.

With your goggles and gloves on, weigh the lye. Sprinkle the lye, little by little, onto the milk. Incorporate it as you go with a big whisk. Don't go too fast, or you'll build up too much heat in one area. Don't go too slowly, or the slush will melt before you get all the lye in. Stir constantly and carefully. The milk will turn pale to bright yellow depending on the kind of milk. If it gets curdled and brown, it has overheated. Although some soapers would just soldier on, you probably want to neutralize it with vinegar and rinse it down the drain. If you get a brown mass, it will smell hideous, so work quickly to take care of it and open up the windows!

If you've been careful with the additions and the temperatures, you will have a lovely yellow solution ready to add to the oils. Keep the temperature of the oils low, about 85°F–90°F, to avoid overheating the milk-lye solution.

USING INFUSIONS

Sometimes you'll want to add a little extra something to make your soap a bit fancier. Any other element added to the liquid—such as plant material, minerals, or mineral pigments used as colorants—will show up in the finished soap in a variety of ways. Some plant matter acts as a natural colorant. Minerals from hard water show up on the surface of the soap as harmless "ash."

If you're using ultramarines or oxides to create a solid color, you can add it right from the start. These mineral pigments stand up perfectly well to the lye, and by making a tinted lye solution, you don't have to worry about specks of undissolved pigment in the soap.

Herbal Infusions

To get the properties of herbs into your soap, infuse them into water or oil. What does that mean? You simply place the herbs in heated water or oil and allow them to steep—as if you're making hot tea. The scents, colors, and beneficial properties of some herbs are strong enough to survive the soapmaking process, but other herbs are not. This is something you'll have to discover for yourself. Many artisanal soapmakers rely on herbal infusions to create their soaps and find that the properties of the herbs come through beautifully.

USING SPICE INFUSIONS IN SOAP

Certain spices release a great amount of color into the solution. Sometimes the lye infusions smell pretty bad, but the scent goes away in the finished soap. Use finely powdered herbs or soft-leaved flakes in this application, as they will be in the final soap and large, hard pieces will scratch.

How to Handle Infusions

Use the infused water just as you would regular water. If you want the texture of the plant material in your soap, don't strain out the herbs before using it. However, there are some herbs that are scratchy on the skin, so be sure to strain those out before using.

Use the infused oils as you would regular oils. Also, use your infused oils right away as the plant matter you've added to it, even if you can't see it, will rot, making the oil unusable.

Since you'll need to heat the water to make the infusion, be sure you allow time for the infusion to cool before mixing it with the lye. Remember you need to use room temperature or colder water to make the lye solution. Depending on the strength of the infusion, adding the lye to it may make it a strange color with an equally strange odor, but that usually fades in the finished soap.

NEUTRALIZING

As mentioned earlier, lye is extremely caustic. When you first add the lye to the liquid, the resulting solution is also extremely caustic. After this lye solution is mixed with the soapmaking oils, however, the soap begins to neutralize, and becomes safe to touch after it has cured. Always wear goggles and rubber gloves when handling lye, lye solutions, raw soap, and fresh soap. If you are in doubt about how neutralized your soap is, err on the side of wearing goggles and gloves even when they're not needed.

Testing for Neutrality

You can test for neutrality of soap in a number of ways. Using phenolphthalein or litmus papers is the most popular. Phenolphthalein is very reliable, inexpensive, and easy to use. You simply place a couple of drops of the solution on the soap you are testing. If the solution turns pink, it is alkaline and therefore still caustic. If it stays clear, it is neutral.

Also, you can purchase litmus tests at your garden center. Papers are fine. Simply place a piece of litmus paper on the soap. Watch the color and measure it against the chart on the package. Soap is "safe" when it registers between 6 and 10 on the pH scale. (Note that litmus paper is difficult to read, and phenolphthalein is the preferred test.)

Caustic Masses

While your soap is curing, test it every so often for neutrality. If your soap is more than two weeks old and is still highly caustic, something went wrong in the measurements. Don't use that soap; dispose of it at a hazardous materials collection site. Find out from your city or county what the proper disposal method is for caustic materials.

Keep a caustic mass contained until you can dispose of it properly. Line a heavy cardboard box with two heavy plastic garbage bags, one inside the other. Fill the box with clay kitty litter deep enough to absorb the mass. Wearing goggles and gloves, pour or scrape the caustic mass into the bags. Add an equal measure of vinegar. If the mass is soupy, add more litter. Label the box and store it in a safe place until you dispose of it.

EVAPORATION DURING CURING

Part of the curing process involves the evaporation of extra water from the bars. Ideally, there should be just enough liquid in the batch to ensure success of the reaction of lye with oils. A 4-ounce bar will lose approximately ¼–½ ounce of water this way. The bar will shrink a little from its original dimensions, but it will stay essentially the same.

When you make opaque hot-process soap, you will notice that the soap is soft when you cut it, compared to neutral cold-process soap. The hot-process soap is neutral, but it can use some curing time to let some water evaporate and harden up. There will be varying degrees of shrinkage with hot-process soap.

Hand-milled soap will probably distort in shape as it dries. The amount of liquid needed to re-liquefy the soap shreds enough to incorporate the ingredients will evaporate as the soap ages. Since the surface of the soap is usually a bit uneven in texture, the water will evaporate at different rates, causing some warping. That's okay; your artisanal soap should look a bit rough and rustic. It will remind you that it's not store-bought. *You* made it.

SOAP ASH

It is very common to find a thin layer of white powder on the top of your batch of soap. This is called "ash," and it is harmless. It is essentially the minerals from the water that have collected on the surface. If you have a thick, sparkly crust on the surface of your soap, you probably have a caustic, lye-heavy batch. But a thin film of white powder isn't a problem.

Using purified water is the main way to limit the formation of ash, but even soap made with distilled water will sometimes have a layer of ash. It can be because of the composition of the lye or the way the ingredients work together, and sometimes there is no identifiable reason.

Placing plastic wrap on the surface of your poured soap is one way to eliminate the ash layer. Let the wrap cling to the surface on its own, rather than pressing, as you can add lumps and bumps to the surface if you push down too far. Peel it away when you are ready to unmold.

You can also remove the ash layer by hand. When you cut your bars, use a cheese planer to cut away the ash. Some soapers set up their cutters to take off the layer during the cutting process. Or you can just leave it. It isn't harmful, and it is an indication that the soap was made by hand, so it will help give your bar a rustic quality. It is ultimately an aesthetic choice.

MAKING SOAP WITHOUT LYE

If all this talk about caustics and lye concerns you, for example if you have small children at home, before you toss this book aside and pick up another hobby, hold on. It's true that all soap contains lye. However, you can avoid the lye challenge altogether by using home soapmaking techniques that use premade soap. For example, you can try the soap-casting technique, in which premade glycerin soap is melted, scented, tinted, and shaped. You can use a home version of hand milling. Or you can purchase premade cold-process

WHERE TO FIND PHENOLPHTHALEIN

Although not always easy to find, it is worth the search for phenolphthalein as it is economical and extremely easy to use. You can find suppliers through the Internet.

soap and re-form it, usually by grating and melting—or "milling"—making additions, and letting it harden.

Soapmaking techniques that do not require the use of lye are wonderful, creative ways to make soap at home. If you have young children, you may feel freer to make soap without the presence of potentially hazardous caustic substances. However, there are multitudes of home soapmakers who do make lye soap and have small children and pets at home. Just follow the safety instructions in this book and you'll be fine.

CHAPTER THREE

COLD-PROCESS SOAPMAKING

Now that you've learned a few of the basic elements of soapmaking, as well as the all-important safety precautions you must take, it's time to start creating some artisan soaps.

There are essentially two ways to create soap: cold process and hot process. In this chapter you'll learn both ways; then we'll look at what you can put into your soaps, as well as the techniques of casting and hand milling.

COLD PROCESS

Cold-process soapmaking is the basic form of handmade, from-scratch soapmaking. It is called "cold" process because there is no cooking involved. Beyond heating the oils enough to liquefy them, there is no heat applied during the creation of the soap. You will make luscious, gorgeous, gentle, bubbly, fine-textured soap with this process. The cold-process soapmaking technique is relatively simple and gets easier with practice. A blend of oils is mixed with a simple solution of lye and water, stirred until thickened, and poured into a mold.

CURING

Like other products made without a lot of preservatives, cold-process soap is prone to spoilage after a number of months. You can extend the life of your soap through careful formulation and storage. It is also essential to dry your soap between uses. Soap that sits in water or is allowed to be in the stream of the shower will melt away rapidly.

HOW LONG WILL YOUR SOAP LAST?

All solid handmade soaps will melt readily in water because the high level of naturally occurring glycerin keeps the bar softer than mass-produced commercial soap from which the glycerin has been removed. Your soap will become longer lasting as it is allowed to dry and cure, but it will never be as long-lasting as the commercial variety.

After cutting and while curing, cold-process soap needs to have a constant temperature and air circulation. Depending on the amount of soap you make, you can dry your soap on a paper-covered cookie sheet, a small shelf, or create an entire curing and drying rack system. However you choose to cure it, be sure to turn it every few days during the first couple of weeks so that it will cure evenly.

Colorant Limitations

The outcome of making cold-process soap is limited in a couple of ways. Lye is not kind to natural colorants. For example, the brilliant ruby-red color that you can infuse into oil with alkanet root will fade to a light pink. The same goes for the bright orange you can get from annatto: It will fade to a color ranging from buttery yellow to subtle orange.

You can, however, get beautiful colors from mineral pigments, food and cosmetic colorants, and micas. Be certain to use colorants that are safe for cosmetic use and stable in cold-process soap. Some micas, although safe in soap, will have their color destroyed by the process. (For further discussion of color, see Chapter 9.)

Scenting Options

In Chapters 7 and 8 you will find a thorough discussion of using both fragrance oils and essential oils to give your artisanal soap a scent. In order to enjoy the delights of essential oils, you must add a relatively large amount to the cold-process soap batter. The general usage rate is approximately ½ ounce of essential oils per 1 pound of base oils. This varies when using absolutes, concretes, and resins.

FIND YOUR FRAGRANCE LEVEL

As a starting point, for each pound of oils used in a batch, you can start with 1 teaspoon of fragrance oil or 1 tablespoon of essential oil. Once you've made a number of batches, you will find the level of fragrance you like.

Fragrance oils that are designed for use in cold-process soap hold up beautifully through the soapmaking process. It is important that you use "soap-safe" fragrance oils. These oils have been tested and selected by suppliers.

When you create blends using both essential oils and fragrance oils, you need to be sure you use the proper measurements for each. Fragrance oil usage is usually about one-third the rate of essential oils. Not all fragrance oils are the same, so be sure you get the manufacturer's or distributor's rate of use for each oil you use.

Unmolding

In cold-process soapmaking, you need a recipe that creates a hard, releasable soap. In Chapter 4, you will find cold-process recipes with additives such as beeswax to help a bar release from a single mold. Some complicated designs need a very hard bar to release at all.

Cold-process soapmaking requires that the soap go through a "gel" phase during its insulation time. In a block mold, the heat generated by the soap mass inside the towel-wrapped, insulated mold will be enough for the soap to get through that phase.

When you pour the soap into a series of three 4-ounce single bars, it is more difficult for the soap to generate enough heat to gel. Help the soap get hot enough by stacking the multicavity molds in a large plastic storage container. Stack them so the soaps above don't sit directly on the open molds below. Put on the lid and wrap the container with towels. If the weather is warm, you can put an insulated box of molds outside in the sun to help it get up to temperature.

STORING COLD-PROCESS SOAPS

After the soap is fully cured, you have a number of storage options. Soap continues to lose water, even after it is fully cured, which makes it harder and longer lasting. It is important to keep the cured soap where air will circulate around it. Try an open cardboard box with a piece of netting over the top to keep the dust out. Be sure the soaps are not too crowded.

Crowding can cause pockets of moisture or oil to build up, which will contribute to spoilage. Additionally, crowding will facilitate scent transfer. In other words, if you store differently scented bars together, they will take on each other's smell.

VARIETIES OF OIL

You can make cold-process soap from a large variety of oils, ranging from a single-oil soap, such as 100 percent olive oil, to a complicated blend of exotic oils. With a little research you can get exactly the texture, hardness, lather quality, cleansing, and moisture benefit you want. You can leave the base recipe plain, or you can enrich it with color, scent, texture, and extra oils for moisturizing.

Eventually, most soap will spoil. The higher the percentage of extra oil in the recipe, the sooner this will happen. You can use preservatives, such as grapefruit seed extract, that are thought to retard spoilage. Your best insurance against spoilage is a correctly formulated recipe that doesn't have a large percentage of excess oil. This, paired with proper curing and storage, will make the soap stay fresh longer. If you plan to sell your soap, it is a good idea to have a clear idea of how long a bar from each recipe will maintain freshness. Do this by saving a new batch for at least six months. Keep records of how it ages.

SOAPMAKING TERMS

It's possible that you're saying to yourself at this point, "Yes, but when do we actually make some soap?" I understand your impatience to begin. We're almost ready.

Before you start your first batch of cold-process artisanal soap, there are some specialized soapmaking terms you need to understand. Most of these terms will apply to the other techniques in this book. You'll find that soapmakers often use these terms, but there is some variation from location to location and process to process.

Mise en place

Mise en place is a term borrowed from French cooking. It refers to the practice of measuring out all the ingredients ahead of time and putting away everything except what you'll be using in your recipe. This is a good habit to get into as a soapmaker. It helps you to get organized and stay focused while you work.

Trace

The term *trace* refers to the presence of traces of the soap mixture on the surface of the mass when some is taken up on your stirrer and dribbled back in. If the dribble makes no mark, your soap has not traced. When it leaves a little lump on the surface that sinks in quickly, it's beginning to trace.

When a soap mixture "traces," it has reached a certain level of saponification. A trace state is described from "light" to "heavy." A soap is said to have reached "full" trace when it is at the state desired to do what you need it to do next. You will add color, scent, and other materials at varying levels of trace. As you gain experience, you'll be able to recognize the signs of trace.

When the oils and lye solution are first mixed, the solution will be transparent, and as you stir, it will become less so. Opacity and a slight graininess lets you know that your soap is tracing. There is also a subtle "soap smell" that comes at the same time.

If you've made gravy or pancake batter, you've experienced the changing texture that many soapers compare to trace. A light trace may be like a thin pancake batter, a medium trace like a medium-thick gravy. If your soap gets gloppy, you've got a heavily traced batch, and you need to get it into its mold as soon as possible.

Trace issues will cease to be issues at all as you make more and more soap. You must stir your soap to trace before pouring. If your soap hasn't traced, it will likely separate and remain unsaponified in layers of oils and lye solution. There are some recipes that have special trace needs, and they are indicated in the recipe instructions.

Saponification

Saponification is another essential of soapmaking vocabulary. It means "to turn into soap." The reaction between the lye solution and the oils is called saponification. Saponification starts as soon as the lye solution and oils come into contact. The liquid, such as water or milk, for example, facilitates the reaction by making sure all the various molecules get together.

The saponification process continues until all the alkali and fatty acids (the lye and the oils) have reacted. In cold-process soapmaking, this can take a few weeks or more. As the soap ages, the reaction slows down considerably, and eventually no unreacted alkali remains. "Young" soap will still have some alkalinity, which decreases as the soap ages.

Alkalinity, and acidity as well, is measured on the pH scale. This scale is divided into a range of pH measures from 0 to 14. Substances with low pH factors, such as lye, are "alkalis" or "bases," while those with high pH factors, like vinegar, are "acids." Neutrals are found in the middle, around pH 7. Your soap should have a pH between 6 and 10.

A soap is said to be "fully saponified" when there is exactly enough oil and lye to fully react. Since you usually want a little extra oil in your soap, for gentleness and moisturizing benefit, most soaps are formulated with slightly more oil than will completely saponify.

Superfatting

This is called "lye discount" or *superfatting*. You may create a gentler soap by calculating a lye discount into your recipe. A lye discount is a reduction from the total amount of lye needed to saponify the oils. When you superfat to create a gentler soap, you add extra oils at the end of the stir before you pour. Overly lye-discounted or superfatted soap is softer and prone to rapid spoilage. Lye-heavy soap is a worse problem, as it makes harsh, caustic, and unusable soap.

The lye soap recipes in this book are created with a 5–7 percent lye discount, and most of them contain one or more superfatting agents. If you want to add more superfatting agents, keep it to 1 tablespoon per pound of oils, or you'll get soap that is soft and spoils more quickly.

CLEAN UP

It is a good idea to clean up as you go. With lye soaps, use the kitchen sink to corral the lye-touched objects as you finish with them. Rinse the lye-pouring pitcher with water and a splash of vinegar, then fill it partway with water and more vinegar so you can place the other things in a neutralizing bath.

GETTING STARTED

For your first cold-process batch, here is an excellent blend of basic soapmaking oils for a 1-pound recipe. This is an unscented, uncolored soap recipe; you should become familiar with this process before moving on to the scented and colored soaps presented later in this book. You will notice that the total weight comes to 24 ounces. It is called a 1-pound recipe because you are using 1 pound of oil. Additives such as color, scent, and herbs are calculated based on the amount of oils.

For this batch, use two 4-cup glass measuring cups to make the lye solution, heat the oils, and blend the soap. You'll use the first measuring cup for the lye solution, and the second for the oil mixture.

Remember this very important note: *In soapmaking, even when you're using measuring cups for mixing, all of the liquids are weighed on a scale, not measured in a liquid measure!*

WEIGHT OF OILS, NOT BATCH

Soapmakers usually talk in terms of the weight of the oils because the amounts of additives are determined by the quantity of oils, not the total weight of the batch. A 4-pound batch will actually weigh about 6 pounds with the lye and water. An 8-pound batch will weigh about 12 pounds.

BASIC COLD-PROCESS SOAP, 1-POUND BATCH

→ YIELDS APPROXIMATELY 24 OUNCES ←

6 ounces water
2.25 ounces lye

10 ounces olive oil
6 ounces coconut oil

1 tablespoon castor oil

1. Put on all protective gear, including goggles, gloves, and long sleeves.

2. Place the water in a heatproof glass 4-cup measure. Sprinkle the lye slowly and carefully into the water. Stir until dissolved. Set the lye solution aside to cool.

3. Combine the olive oil, coconut oil, and castor oil in a second heatproof glass 4-cup measure. Melt in the microwave or over boiling water. Coconut oil has a low melting point, so it will melt quickly from an opaque white solid to a clear liquid. As each setup is different, be sure to watch your microwave or double boiler closely, and make note of how long it takes. (Do not overheat, as oils take longer to cool than the lye solution.) Set the oils aside to cool.

4. When both mixtures are at 110°F, pour the lye solution in a thin stream into the oils. Stir constantly until the mixture traces, about 10–20 minutes. (If using an immersion blender, take care not to whip air into the mixture.)

5. When the soap batter traces, pour it into the mold, taking care to scrape all the traced soap out of the cup.

6. Cover the mold with plastic wrap, wrap the mold in a towel for warmth, and let it sit for 2 days.

7. Wearing your goggles and gloves, try unmolding the soap by pulling out the sides of the mold and turning the mold upside down on a brown paper bag or paper towel on the work surface. Push on the bottom of the mold. If the soap does not release readily, place the mold in the freezer for 1 hour. Try again to remove it. It should release easily this time.

8. Using a stainless steel knife, cut the soap log into bars. Place them on a brown paper bag to dry. Turn them daily to be sure they dry evenly.

9. In 4 weeks, your soap will be mild and quite firm and ready to use.

10. Store the soap in a ventilated container.

This is your first batch of cold-processed lye soap! Congratulations! When you take it to the tub or shower, observe the smell, texture, lather, and rinsability. Although every bath with your own soap is a learning experience, be sure to take time to enjoy what you've created!

Make sure to add your observations to your soapmaking journal. The more notes you take, the more your learning process will be reinforced. Be sure to write your notes right away so you don't forget!

It is very likely that you'll want to make more soap as soon as possible. Make more of the 1-pound batches from Chapter 4 to start out with. It is tempting to dive right in and go for larger batches, but resist that temptation. Try your mettle on a few smaller batches, then wallow in happiness when they're all cured and ready to use.

TAKING THE NEXT STEP

When you are ready to make a larger batch, try one of the 4-pound recipes in Chapter 4. There are some procedural differences from the 1-pound methods, so try a plain, or at least very simple, batch before committing yourself to enough additives for a batch at the bigger size.

When you make a large batch of plain soap, you can use it as usual, of course. And what's even more fun is that you can use it for the hand-milling recipes in the book. It is much easier and more economical to make your own soap shreds for hand milling than to buy them.

REWARDS FOR WAITING

Cold-process soap is prized for its fine, solid texture. Although it takes four weeks for cold-process soap to cure from the pouring to the ready-to-use stage, it is well worth the wait. The firm bar will have a silky texture and lovely lather, and it will thoroughly and gently clean your skin.

Cooling the Lye

The primary difference between small and larger batches is the amount of time it takes for the lye to cool. Many soapers make their lye solution in the morning, go about their day, then make soap later in the day. Cooling time is affected by the size and shape of your lye container and the relative heat of the day.

The more surface area your lye container has, the faster it will cool. It's better to have an oversized pitcher than one that will be so deeply full that it will take ages to cool. Leaving the lid off the pitcher will help with cooling. You need to be patient and monitor how long it takes so you can plan for the future.

Some soapers find it useful to cool lye outside. If you do cool your lye outside, be sure the pitcher is covered with either its lid or a piece of paper towel, paper, or cardboard square. All kinds of things fall from the sky, such as dust or leaves, and don't forget about those birds flying overhead!

It is essential that you clearly mark the pitcher of cooling lye for what it is. This is important even if you think no one will find it. Better to make a sign no one will read than not to tell the surprise visitor.

The 4-Pound Batch

Don't be intimidated by a bigger batch. A bigger batch just means bigger fun and rewards. You can stir the soap to a light trace, divide it into smaller amounts, and make different varieties from one big batch. You will of course have the same base, but you can get very creative with your additives and have very different soaps from one large batch!

SUZANNE BUCKLES`S FAVORITE 1-POUND RECIPE

Suzanne Buckles has been experimenting with soap recipes for many years. Her generous advice on Internet soapmaking message boards has helped innumerable soapmakers—novices and experts alike. Get some inspiration for your budding soap fascination from her.

5 ounces water
1.9 ounces lye
4.5 ounces palm kernel oil

4.5 ounces coconut oil
4 ounces olive oil

0.5 ounces essential oil or fragrance oil

1. Put on all protective gear, including goggles, gloves, and long sleeves.

2. Place the water in a heatproof glass 4-cup measure. Sprinkle the lye slowly and carefully into the water. Stir until dissolved. Set the lye solution aside to cool.

3. Combine the palm kernel oil, coconut oil, and olive oil in a second heatproof glass 4-cup measure. Melt in the microwave or over boiling water. (Do not overheat, as oils take longer to cool than the lye solution.) Set the oils aside to cool.

4. When both mixtures are at 110°F, pour the lye solution in a thin stream into the oils. Stir constantly until the mixture traces, about 10–20 minutes. If using an immersion blender, it will take about 1 minute. With an immersion blender, take care not to whip air into the mixture. Add the essential oil and blend thoroughly.

5. When the soap batter traces, pour it into the mold, taking care to scrape all the traced soap out of the cup.

6. Cover the mold with plastic wrap, wrap the mold in a towel for warmth, and let it sit for 2 days.

7. Wearing your goggles and gloves, try unmolding the soap by pulling out the sides of the mold and turning the mold upside down on a brown paper bag or paper towel on the work surface. Push on the bottom of the mold. If the soap does not release readily, place the mold in the freezer for 1 hour. Try again. It should release easily this time.

8. Using a stainless steel knife, cut the soap log into bars. Place them on a brown paper bag to dry. Turn them daily to be sure they dry evenly.

9. In 4 weeks, your soap will be mild and quite firm and ready to use.

10. Store the soap in a ventilated container.

VARYING THE COLD PROCESS

As you gain experience with materials, processes, and procedures, you will find ways to customize the basics to suit your own style. The variations on process discussed in this section are best saved for a time when you have gained considerable experience with more customary materials and processes.

Room-Temperature Cold Process

One of the patience-trying parts of learning to make cold-process soap is waiting for the lye to cool to the suggested working temperature and then getting the oils warmed and melted to the same temperature. Rather than waiting for the heat—energy—to dispel, it makes sense to use the idea of an energy exchange—to use the heat of the lye and water reaction to melt and warm the oils. This procedure is called room-temperature cold process.

The success of this alternative cold-process technique depends on many factors. The temperature of the working area has an impact on how the energy exchange occurs, as does the consistency of oils that are sensitive to temperature. A colder room temperature means that coconut oil and shea and other butters take more energy to become liquid and therefore able to be incorporated into the mixture. If your workspace is very cold and you are making small amounts of soap with a large percentage of solid oils, there may not be enough heat energy generated to melt them.

Conversely, if your working area is quite warm, you may end up with more energy than is needed and have a soap mixture that is too warm. When the soap mixture is too warm, it can trace too quickly, or even seize completely. A worst-case scenario, which is thankfully very unusual, is for the soap mixture to "volcano" up and out of the soap pot.

Scent materials that at lower temperatures don't accelerate trace may do so under these conditions. The only way to know what is going to happen is to try it and be prepared to get the soap into the molds quickly.

CLEANING UP

Don't rinse large blobs of gooey soap, either finished or unsaponified, down your drains. They will clog up your drains almost immediately and take a lot to clean out once clogged. Your best bet is to use smart cleanup techniques.

Cold-process soapmaking requires more care with cleanup than the other techniques. Since the soap is caustic all the way through the process and for a few weeks after, always wear goggles and gloves while handling it. Keep track of all the utensils and equipment that you've used with the lye.

After you're finished with a lye-touched tool, place it in the sink, ideally into a container of vinegar and water. If you add water to the sink, be sure not to hit it with a hard stream that will splatter. Keep adding the utensils as you finish using them, pouring vinegar on them as you go.

After you've scraped the last of the beautiful soap batter into the mold, wipe the inside of the pan and any other tools you've used. You can use paper towels, but you'll go through a lot of them. A better idea is to get towels out of the rag bag and tear them into paper towel–sized soap cleanup towels.

You can use your soap cleanup towels over and over, saving money and resources. Place the towels in a plastic bag for a day or two, then add them to the wash. The soap will have saponified enough for laundry use and will contribute to the cleansing.

CHAPTER FOUR

COLD-PROCESS RECIPES

Once you've mastered the basics of cold-process soapmaking, you are ready to experiment and expand your repertoire. From the perfection of an exquisite base recipe to the intricate stripes of a highly contrasted multiple pour, you'll have lots of fun creating and learning!

CREATING THE PERFECT BASIC BAR

Once you've mastered the basic techniques, you can begin to manipulate the ratios of oils to create exactly the properties you desire. Increasing one oil, eliminating another, replacing one for another—all these experiments will lead you to your perfect basic bar.

The recipes provided in this chapter offer a variety of bases. Differences in kinds and ratios of oils make different sorts of soaps. Remember that these recipes have been formulated with the purpose of inspiring you to create your own formulas. If you don't want to make your own formulas, these will, of course, provide you with enough variety to keep you busy!

Recipe Sizing

The recipes that follow are given in four manageable sizes. As noted in the previous chapter, the amounts used to describe them refer, as always, to the number of pounds of oils, not the size of the whole batch. Additives are, for the most part, measured according to pounds of oils in a batch, so it's easier and clearer to refer to a batch by how many pounds of oils are in it.

There will be a slight variation from "exactly" 1-pound, 2-pound, 4-pound, and 8-pound batches. Formulating for exactly 16 ounces can make the amount of lye difficult to measure on a standard scale with ¼-ounce increments, so some 1-pound batches will have, for example, 17 ounces.

Equipment

The equipment you use for your soap pot and lye solution container will change depending on the size batch you are making. For the 1-pound batches, heatproof 4-cup glass measures work perfectly for mixing the lye, warming the oils, and mixing them together. You'll pour the lye solution into the cup already holding the oils, and mix and pour from it as well.

For the 2-, 4-, and 8-pound batches, an 8-quart stainless steel stock pot works great for warming the oils and mixing. For the lye solution for those batches, you'll need a 4-quart pitcher. Be sure the pitcher is heat safe! It must be able to withstand nearly boiling temperatures.

It must have a secure lid and have a sturdy handle. Many soapers use glass juice bottles, milk bottles, and other glass containers. A plastic pitcher with a handle is easy to lift and doesn't get as hot. Also, it won't shatter if you drop it. (The heavy heatproof glass 4-cup measure is fine for the 1-pound batches because you're only using 6 ounces of water.)

CHOOSE THE SIZE

CHOOSE THE SIZE

For each of the recipes that follow, choose the size batch you want to make. That will tell you how much of each ingredient you need. Then follow the instructions for making Basic Cold-Process Soap, 1-Pound Batch in Chapter 3.

Base Recipes

Choose a base recipe that contains oils you can get easily. You can make serviceable soap with vegetable shortening, lard, soy oil, olive oil, and other easy-to-obtain oils. It is worth it, though, to go to the extra trouble to find other oils, especially coconut oil and castor oil. You can make an excellent bar with olive oil and coconut oil with a bit of castor oil for superfatting. Start with 1-pound batches to help you conserve materials and increase your familiarity with the procedures.

Ingredients	1-pound batch *(about 1½ pounds total weight)*	2-pound batch *(about 3 pounds total weight)*	4-pound batch *(about 6 pounds total weight)*	8-pound batch *(about 12 pounds total weight)*
Lye solution				
Water	6 ounces	12 ounces	1 pound 8 ounces	3 pounds
Lye	2 ounces	4 ounces	8.25 ounces	1 pound 0.75 ounces
Base oil				
Olive oil	1 pound	2 pounds	4 pounds	8 pounds
Superfat				
Castor oil	1 tablespoon	2 tablespoons	4 tablespoons	8 tablespoons
Additives				
Color				
Scent material	Total 1 tablespoon EO or 2 teaspoons FO	Total 2 tablespoons EO or 2 teaspoons FO	Total 4 tablespoons EO or 4 teaspoons FO	Total 8 tablespoons EO or 8 teaspoons FO
Herbs				
Other				

(EO is essential oil; FO is fragrance oil)

SOYBEAN SHORTENING

Check the label to be sure it is 100 percent soy. This soap will be soft and have a low lather.

However, it works well and is extremely inexpensive.

Ingredients	1-pound batch *(about 1½ pounds total weight)*	2-pound batch *(about 3 pounds total weight)*	4-pound batch *(about 6 pounds total weight)*	8-pound batch *(about 12 pounds total weight)*
Lye solution				
Lye	2 ounces	4 ounces	8.25 ounces	16.5 ounces
Water	6 ounces	12 ounces	1 pound 8 ounces	3 pounds
Oil				
Soybean shortening	1 pound	2 pounds	4 pounds	8 pounds

OLIVE OIL

Olive oil soap is also known as Castile soap.

Ingredients	1-pound batch *(about 1½ pounds total weight)*	2-pound batch *(about 3 pounds total weight)*	4-pound batch *(about 6 pounds total weight)*	8-pound batch *(about 12 pounds total weight)*
Lye solution				
Lye	2 ounces	4 ounces	8.25 ounces	1 pound 0.75 ounces
Water	6 ounces	12 ounces	1 pound 8 ounces	3 pounds
Oil				
Olive oil	1 pound	2 pounds	4 pounds	8 pounds

OLIVE OIL AND COCONUT OIL

This is the ratio used by some of the best soapers around. It is hard and has great lather.

Ingredients	1-pound batch *(about 1½ pounds total weight)*	2-pound batch *(about 3 pounds total weight)*	4-pound batch *(about 6 pounds total weight)*	8-pound batch *(about 12 pounds total weight)*
Lye solution				
Lye	2.4 ounces	4.8 ounces	9.7 ounces	1 pound 3.4 ounces
Water	6 ounces	12 ounces	1 pound 8 ounces	3 pounds
Oil blend				
Olive oil	10.5 ounces	1 pound 5 ounces	2 pounds 10 ounces	5 pounds 4 ounces
Coconut oil	5.25 ounces	10.5 ounces	1 pound 5 ounces	2 pounds 10 ounces
Superfat				
Castor oil	1 tablespoon	2 tablespoons	4 tablespoons	8 tablespoons

OLIVE OIL, COCONUT OIL, AND LARD

Ingredients	1-pound batch *(about 1½ pounds total weight)*	2-pound batch *(about 3 pounds total weight)*	4-pound batch *(about 6 pounds total weight)*	8-pound batch *(about 12 pounds total weight)*
Lye solution				
Lye	2.3 ounces	4.6 ounces	9.2 ounces	1 pound 2 ounces
Water	6 ounces	12 ounces	1 pound 8 ounces	3 pounds
Oil blend				
Olive oil	6 ounces	12 ounces	1 pound 8 ounces	3 pounds
Coconut oil	5 ounces	10 ounces	1 pound 4 ounces	2 pounds 8 ounces
Lard	5 ounces	10 ounces	1 pound 4 ounces	2 pounds 8 ounces
Superfat				
Castor oil	1 tablespoon	2 tablespoons	4 tablespoons	8 tablespoons

OLIVE OIL, COCONUT OIL, AND PALM OIL

Ingredients	1-pound batch *(about 1½ pounds total weight)*	2-pound batch *(about 3 pounds total weight)*	4-pound batch *(about 6 pounds total weight)*	8-pound batch *(about 12 pounds total weight)*
Lye solution				
Lye	2.4 ounces	4.8 ounces	9.6 ounces	1 pound 3 ounces
Water	6 ounces	12 ounces	1 pound 8 ounces	3 pounds
Oil blend				
Olive oil	9 ounces	1 pound 2 ounces	2 pounds 4 ounces	4 pounds 8 ounces
Coconut oil	4 ounces	8 ounces	1 pound	2 pounds
Palm oil	3 ounces	6 ounces	12 ounces	1 pound 8 ounces
Superfat				
Castor oil	1 tablespoon	2 tablespoons	4 tablespoons	8 tablespoons

OLIVE OIL, COCONUT OIL, AND PALM KERNEL OIL

Ingredients	1-pound batch *(about 1½ pounds total weight)*	2-pound batch *(about 3 pounds total weight)*	4-pound batch *(about 6 pounds total weight)*	8-pound batch *(about 12 pounds total weight)*
Lye solution				
Lye	2.25 ounces	4.5 ounces	9 ounces	1 pound 2 ounces
Water	6 ounces	12 ounces	1 pound 8 ounces	3 pounds
Oil blend				
Olive oil	9.5 ounces	1 pound 3 ounces	2 pounds 6 ounces	4 pounds 12 ounces
Coconut oil	5 ounces	10 ounces	1 pound 4 ounces	2 pounds 8 ounces
Palm kernel oil	1.5 ounces	3 ounces	6 ounces	12 ounces
Superfat				
Castor oil	1 tablespoon	2 tablespoons	4 tablespoons	8 tablespoons

SOY OIL, COCONUT OIL, AND PALM KERNEL OIL

Soy oil is inexpensive and readily available.

Ingredients	1-pound batch *(about 1½ pounds total weight)*	2-pound batch *(about 3 pounds total weight)*	4-pound batch *(about 6 pounds total weight)*	8-pound batch *(about 12 pounds total weight)*
Lye solution				
Lye	2.4 ounces	4.8 ounces	9.6 ounces	1 pound 3 ounces
Water	6 ounces	12 ounces	1 pound 8 ounces	3 pounds
Oil blend				
Soy oil	9 ounces	1 pound 2 ounces	2 pounds 4 ounces	4 pounds 8 ounces
Coconut oil	4 ounces	8 ounces	1 pound	2 pounds
Palm kernel oil	3 ounces	6 ounces	12 ounces	1 pound 8 ounces
Superfat				
Castor oil	1 tablespoon	2 tablespoons	4 tablespoons	8 tablespoons

STANDARD RECIPES

Using the following standard—or classic—recipes, you'll select scent and color additives to make two all-time soap favorites: oatmeal and lavender. These soap recipes use fragrance oils (FO) or essential oils (EO) or combinations of both. They have basic additives and simple coloring techniques. Use the suggested amounts of additives as a guide to making your own simple recipes.

OATMEAL

Ingredients	1-pound batch *(about 1½ pounds total weight)*	2-pound batch *(about 3 pounds total weight)*	4-pound batch *(about 6 pounds total weight)*	8-pound batch *(about 12 pounds total weight)*
Additive	1 tablespoon finely ground oatmeal	2 tablespoons finely ground oatmeal	4 tablespoons finely ground oatmeal	8 tablespoons finely ground oatmeal
Scent material	1 teaspoon Oatmeal, Milk, and Honey FO	2 teaspoons Oatmeal, Milk, and Honey FO	1 tablespoon + 1 teaspoon Oatmeal, Milk, and Honey FO	2 tablespoons + 2 teaspoons Oatmeal, Milk, and Honey FO

LAVENDER

Ingredients	1-pound batch *(about 1½ pounds total weight)*	2-pound batch *(about 3 pounds total weight)*	4-pound batch *(about 6 pounds total weight)*	8-pound batch *(about 12 pounds total weight)*
Colorant	½ teaspoon ultramarine violet	1 teaspoon ultramarine violet	2 teaspoons ultramarine violet	1 tablespoon + 1 teaspoon ultramarine violet
Scent material	1 tablespoon Lavender EO	2 tablespoons Lavender EO	4 tablespoons Lavender EO	8 tablespoons Lavender EO

EXOTIC RECIPES

The following recipes venture from the perfectly wonderful world of soaps made from "common" oils into the more costly world of exotic oils. These exotic oils can be more expensive, so be sure you know what you're doing. And if you experiment, use a 1-pound batch.

~ SHEA BUTTER COMBO ~

Ingredients	1-pound batch *(about 1½ pounds total weight)*	2-pound batch *(about 3 pounds total weight)*	4-pound batch *(about 6 pounds total weight)*	8-pound batch *(about 12 pounds total weight)*
Lye solution				
Lye	2.4 ounces	4.8 ounces	9.6 ounces	1 pound 3 ounces
Water	6 ounces	12 ounces	1 pound 8 ounces	3 pounds
Oil blend				
Shea butter	2 ounces	4 ounces	8 ounces	1 pound
Almond oil	4 ounces	8 ounces	1 pound	2 pounds
Olive oil	5 ounces	10 ounces	1 pound 4 ounces	2 pounds 8 ounces
Coconut oil	5 ounces	10 ounces	1 pound 4 ounces	2 pounds 8 ounces
Superfat				
Castor oil	1 tablespoon	2 tablespoons	4 tablespoons	8 tablespoons

AVOCADO-MANGO COMBO

Ingredients	1-pound batch *(about 1½ pounds total weight)*	2-pound batch *(about 3 pounds total weight)*	4-pound batch *(about 6 pounds total weight)*	8-pound batch *(about 12 pounds total weight)*
Lye solution				
Lye	2.4 ounces	4.8 ounces	9.6 ounces	1 pound 3 ounces
Water	6 ounces	12 ounces	1 pound 8 ounces	3 pounds
Oil blend				
Avocado oil	3 ounces	6 ounces	12 ounces	1 pound 8 ounces
Mango butter	3 ounces	6 ounces	12 ounces	1 pound 8 ounces
Coconut oil	5 ounces	10 ounces	1 pound 4 ounces	2 pounds 8 ounces
Olive oil	5 ounces	10 ounces	1 pound 4 ounces	2 pounds 8 ounces
Superfat				
Castor oil	1 tablespoon	2 tablespoons	4 tablespoons	8 tablespoons

LAYERING SOAPS

Layering entails any of the following: two color layers, fused together; two separate textures joined with a third, contrasting layer; and fancy slanted patterning. Layering is done in at least two steps. In a half-and-half layer pattern, you make and pour one half of the volume of the mold. Let the first half sit long enough so that the second layer will sit on top of it. Then make and pour the second layer, which is the other half of the volume. The layers bond and fuse through the heat of the insulation period.

TILTING THE MOLD

You can tilt the mold one way for the first layer, then another way for the following layers for an angled effect in the cut bars. Be sure you don't tip the mold so far that the soap pours out. Also, make sure that the first layer is totally firm before you tilt for the next layer.

When you're working with three or more layers, you'll need to make and pour the layers at higher temperatures to be sure that the soap will go through the gel phase. It may take some experimenting with times to find what works best for your climate and ambient temperature.

SWIRLING AND MARBLING SOAPS

The creation of beautiful designs through swirling and marbling is an art in itself. Getting the soap to just the right texture, stage of trace, and temperature takes practice. Learning how much to stir (not too little, not too much), understanding the relationship between the direction of a "pull" and the way you cut the soap, and endless variation, chance, and willingness to embrace the unexpected are hallmarks of a successful application of these techniques.

CONTROLLING THE SWIRLS

You can control the swirls and marbling effects by the heaviness of the trace at which you pour the colors together. You'll get a more fluid, thinner swirl if you pour at a thin-to-medium trace. If you pour when the soap batter is more heavily traced, you'll get bigger portions of color.

Swirling

Prepare all colorants ahead and stir them before using in case they've settled while you've been setting up.

Be sure that you know if the scent material you use will accelerate trace. If it does at one temperature and doesn't at another, use the temperature that won't contribute to the acceleration.

SWIRLING ALL THROUGH

Using shallow molds—two bars thick, for example—helps ensure that the swirling pattern goes all the way through the soap. Be sure to cut the soap so that the design shows on the long, broad sides of the bars.

If you want to work with a thin soap batter to get tiny details in the swirls, you must be sure it is actually traced. Experience is the only way to be able to make this determination. The line between not traced and lightly traced is thin, and it's not easy to recognize until you've had some experience. Refinement of technique comes through experience. When you are working on something challenging, try to go through with it and don't fear "failure." The worst thing that will happen is that you'll lose a batch of soap. Keeping batches small can help you maintain perspective.

Working in a set pattern makes the swirls more specific. Depending on the thickness of the soap batter, use a chopstick, flexible plastic spoon, narrow spatula, or other tool you find useful. Drag the tool back and forth lengthwise through the soap, making sure to get to the bottom of the mold. Then do the same thing widthwise. This should do it. There is a temptation to continue to work the pattern, but it may just blend the soap colors, leaving you with a muddy effect.

For more advanced patterning, make a "comb" with which you can drag a number of lines simultaneously. Fasten about six chopsticks together tightly with a series of rubber bands, spaced at even intervals. Break the chopsticks to a length that will allow you to get to the bottom of the mold and keep your hand above the surface of the soap. Insert your fingers between the chopsticks, spaced evenly.

Beginner's Recipes

Because you have to divide the batter into smaller portions for scenting and coloring, you'll need to blend the lye and oils at about 110°F. Higher temperatures can help to delay trace. Superfat the entire batch before dividing.

LAVENDER GERANIUM RIBBON

The less you stir, the more solid areas of color you'll have.

1 batch of your favorite cold-process recipe, such as Basic Cold-Process Soap,	1-Pound Batch (see Chapter 3) Lavender essential oil	Rose geranium essential oil Ultramarine violet Ultramarine pink

1. Make a batch of your favorite cold-process recipe. Pour at 110°F to be sure you have enough time to divide and color the batch. Add the essential oils.

2. When it is still at a light trace, divide the batch in half. Color one half with the violet ultramarine and the other with pink ultramarine. Stir both batches to medium trace and pour the pink into the purple.

3. Without stirring, pour into the mold. Insulate well and let sit for 2 days. Unmold as usual.

CLOUDY SKIES

For this recipe, scent the entire batch and then color half with the blue colorant.

| 1 batch of your favorite cold-process recipe, such as Basic Cold-Process Soap, | 1-Pound Batch (see Chapter 3) | Ocean rain fragrance oil Ultramarine blue |

1. Make a batch of your favorite cold-process recipe. Scent the entire batch and then color half with the blue colorant. Pour both parts back into your soap pot.

2. *Do not stir.* Pour in a circular motion into a block mold. The pouring action will cause the soap to marble.

Swirling in Bar Molds

As you've seen, swirling in block molds creates soaps you can cut into bars or even form into spheres if you cut the soap when it's soft enough. The results are unpredictable and cutting the bars is always like opening a surprise present.

You can also make swirls and marble effects in individual bar molds. Finding just the right combination of mold, color, and intensity of swirl can create a magnificent bar! It can take some time and trial and error, but even an "ugly" bar is still a treasure.

You need to have enough molds on hand to hold the batch. For example, if your molds have three cavities each, and each cavity holds 4 ounces, you'll need four trays to hold the whole batch. Have an extra mold on hand to pour any extra soap into. Don't let good soap batter go to waste!

BEESWAX TO UNMOLD

In order to help your soap release from the molds, you may need to tweak your recipe a little. It's very easy! Adding 1 teaspoon of melted beeswax per pound of oils to the warmed/melted oils will take care of any possible release problems.

GOLD AND BLUE DOLPHINS

1 batch of your favorite cold-process recipe, such as Basic Cold-Process Soap, 1-Pound Batch (see Chapter 3)

1 teaspoon beeswax per pound of oils

Gold mica
Your favorite blue coloring

1. Make a batch of your desired recipe in a size to fit the bar molds you have. Add the beeswax to the oils when you melt them. (This will ensure ease of release from the molds.)

2. Divide the batch equally into two containers you can easily pour from. (Pyrex measuring cups work very well.) Color one with lots of gold mica and the other with the blue coloring.

3. Simultaneously pour both colors into each cavity of the mold. With these dolphins, you can try some where you pour the surface of each dolphin a different color.

Marbling

The creation of exquisite marbling effects can become both quest and obsession. We can look to the world of paper marbling and faux-finishing for techniques. Laying out the colors then manipulating them into the elaborate swirls, feathers, and shells works for soap in a way similar to paper marbling, but instead of transferring the design to paper or fabric, you want the design to penetrate to below the surface. Getting this to happen is a matter of practice and know-how.

It's not possible to cover all variables as they vary from soapmaker to soapmaker, recipe to recipe, mold to mold, and more. But here are some observations from experience, research, and practice:

· The more fluid the soap, the finer and more detailed the swirls.

· The thicker the soap, the coarser the swirls.

· Thickly traced colored soap will sink through a less-traced base, allowing for mold-deep pattern, but it can be much harder to shape into a pattern.

- The deeper the mold, the more difficult it is to get the pattern all the way through the soap.

- Surface ash that will obscure the pattern can be avoided by covering the surface of the poured soap with plastic film.

- Be sure to stir each color thoroughly just before pouring or you may end up with unevenly saponified ribbons that fall away from the rest of the soap.

Selecting a Mold

To make marbled soap, select a mold and recipe size that will give you a depth of about 2½–3". An easy way to find out how much soap to make, or how much you'll be using of a batch you usually make, is to select a wide, shallow mold and fill it with water to the desired depth. Weigh that water to determine the approximate weight of the soap batter you'll need to get the depth you want.

Making a Trial Run Shallow Mold

Needing a specifically sized mold is a good time to try out mold sizes that are uniquely yours. You can make or have made wooden molds that you'll use for years. They can be expensive in time and money, so making a trial version of the shape you think you want is a great idea. Measure and weigh a bar of soap that you want to use as a model for the bars you'll get from your mold. For example, a 4-ounce bar that measures ½" deep, 3" long, and 2" wide. Use a sheet of foam-core board to make your trial mold. You're basically making a box with no top. Draw a rectangle in the center of the board, leaving room for the side flaps.

HEATING FOR LONGER LIFE

As a general rule, combining the lye and oils between 105°F and 110°F will help keep your soap fluid longer. This is not always the case; it depends on your formula and additives.

When you have the lines drawn, use a craft knife and a metal straightedge to cut through the top layer of paper and the foam, stopping short of cutting through the other side. (You're not actually cutting the rectangle out, just scoring the paper and foam to make it easier to fold up the sides.) You'll have a big rectangle with four flaps. Turn the board over and fold up the sides. Secure the corners with packing tape. Line the mold with freezer paper to make it easy to lift out the block without destroying your trial mold, in case you want to keep using it.

Make up a batch of your favorite cold-process formula. You don't have to limit the batch to your target mold; you can use part of it in that mold and part of it in another. This freedom from worry over getting it exactly right can be very empowering and give you a chance to try out other ingredients from the same big batch.

CHUNKING SOAPS

Chunked soaps are made in at least two stages. The first stage is to make soap in one or more colors and let it harden for a few days. Then you cut that soap into chunks and place them in the mold. Next, you make more soap and pour it over the chunks. When you cut the soap, the cross-section of the chunks and the over-pour makes a pretty and unique design in each bar.

By adding texture and color variety to the chunk batch, you add even more excitement to your creation. You can make the chunks in single colors, swirls, and layers. The addition of spices, seeds, or herbs adds even more visual interest.

Starting Out

These projects take some time and planning. You need to make the chunk soap about 5 days ahead. This is long enough for it to set so that it can be cut into pieces, and short enough so it will still bind easily to the soap poured over it.

Since you'll be working with small amounts of soap for the contrasts, you need to be doubly sure of your measurements. The following recipes are for 4-pound batches. You'll make 1 or 2 pounds first for contrasts, then the remaining 2–3 pounds for the over-pour.

For the smaller chunk batches, you'll need to work with higher temperatures than usual. The higher temperature will give you more time for multiple

manipulations and will start the batch off with enough heat to help it get through the gel phase.

You will then cut the first part of the batch into the desired shapes. When you cut the chunk soap into pieces, you can get creative and cut them into specific shapes if you wish. Choose molds that will help you create the shapes of the chunks you'd like to make.

Add the chunks to the over-pour, stir carefully and well, and then pour the whole thing into the mold. Use a chopstick to be sure that there are no hidden air pockets and that the chunks are placed in the mold where you want them to be.

Chunking Recipes

The following recipes are done in stages. They are based on a 4-pound oil-based recipe because that size is easy to handle. You can, of course, make the batches smaller or larger. Use any base recipe you want. It is a good idea to use the same base recipe for all stages of the multiphase recipe.

GINGER-PAPAYA

Ginger-papaya fragrance oil is available at Symphony Scents.

4 pounds of your favorite cold-process recipe, such as Basic Cold-Process Soap, 1-pound batch (see Chapter 3), divided

Ginger-papaya fragrance oil
Bright papaya orange colorant

Leafy green colorant
2 teaspoons poppy seeds

1. Make 2 pounds of soap, and scent with the fragrance oil. Divide equally into two separate mixing cups at trace. Color one half bright papaya orange and the other a leafy green.

2. Pour, insulate, and cure for a day or two. Cut the orange batch into cubes and the green batch into thinner pieces.

3. Make 2 more pounds of soap, and scent with the fragrance oil. Do not color, but add the poppy seeds. Add the orange and green chunks to the soap pot and stir carefully to coat all the pieces. Pour at thick trace into the mold.

MELON SALAD

PART ONE: CHUNKS IN THREE COLORS

Cubes of green, pink, and pale orange soap scented with a triple-melon fragrance oil blend, with an off-white over-pour.

2 pounds of your favorite cold-process recipe, such as Basic Cold-Process Soap, 1-pound batch (see Chapter 3)

Watermelon fragrance oil
Cantaloupe fragrance oil
Honeydew fragrance oil
¼ teaspoon titanium dioxide

Pinch red oxide
⅛ teaspoon ultramarine pink
⅛ teaspoon chromium green

1. Make a 2-pound batch, add the watermelon fragrance oil, cantaloupe fragrance oil, honeydew fragrance oil, and titanium dioxide, and divide it equally into three mixing cups.

2. Mix 1 tablespoon of the soap batter from each mixing cup with each colorant and stir into the cups. Color one part with red oxide, one with ultramarine pink, and one with chromium green.

3. Pour into small block molds. Insulate well for 2 days. Unmold and cut into cubes. Let cure for 3 days.

PART TWO: OVER-POUR

2 pounds of your favorite cold-process recipe, such as Basic Cold-Process Soap, 1-Pound Batch (see Chapter 3)

Watermelon fragrance oil
Cantaloupe fragrance oil

Honeydew fragrance oil

1. Make a 2-pound batch and scent with the watermelon fragrance oil, cantaloupe fragrance oil, and honeydew fragrance oil.

2. Add the colored chunks from part 1 to the pan and stir well, coating all the surfaces.

3. Pour into the mold. Use a chopstick to get rid of any air bubbles and arrange the chunks the way you want them.

4. Insulate well and let sit for 2 days. Unmold and cut into bars as desired.

SALT BARS

Salt bars are a hybrid between soap and bath salts, and are both easy to make and very popular. They are not scrubby, except perhaps at first, but smooth with use as the initial sharp edges begin to resemble smooth stone. They have a silky, lotion-like lather and leave you feeling clean and refreshed.

To create salt bars, you can make up a batch of soap as usual, and then stir the salt of your choice into the lightly traced soap batter after adding fragrance and color. The soap will begin to solidify and heat up as soon as the salt is added. You'll have to get the soap batter into the mold quickly or it will solidify in the mixing container. The soap will reach a high temperature quickly, so you don't need to insulate it. Cut the batch into bars as soon as it is cool, or it may get too hard to cut.

Confetti Soap

An easy and visually appealing version of chunking is called confetti. Instead of cutting the contrasting colors into big pieces, shred them with a cheese grater, using the side with the largest holes. Fold the shreds into the base color rather than pouring the base color on top.

MAKING MILK SOAPS

Of all the ways there are to make milk soap, the most effective one requires working with frozen milk. If you add lye to room temperature milk, it will curdle and turn brown, becoming a hideous, stinky mess. You also need to work with oils that are as cool as they can be without resolidifying.

HALF-AND-HALF VANILLA DELUXE

This rich, creamy soap is a luxurious delight. Special Edition Vanilla from Sweet Cakes not only makes the soap smell incredibly delicious, it also colors the soap a warm vanilla-bean brown.

➤ YIELDS APPROXIMATELY 24 OUNCES ◀

10 ounces olive oil

6 ounces coconut oil

6 ounces half-and-half, frozen

2.25 ounces lye

2 teaspoons Sweet Cakes Special Edition Vanilla fragrance oil or your favorite rich vanilla fragrance oil

1 tablespoon castor oil

1. Combine the olive oil and coconut oil in a heatproof glass 4-cup measure. Melt in the microwave or over boiling water. (Do not overheat, as it takes oils longer to cool than the lye solution. You will be combining the lye and oils at a very low temperature.)

2. Place the half-and-half in a wide, deep tempered glass or stainless steel mixing bowl. (The idea is to keep the mixture shallow.) Break up the frozen chunks so the half-and-half is slushy but not melted.

3. Sprinkle the lye *very* slowly and carefully over the slushy half-and-half, stirring constantly. (As you stir, the mixture will become pale yellow. If you add the lye too fast or don't stir as you go, you could end up with an overheated, brown, curdled mess.)

4. Check the temperature of the half-and-half–lye solution. Let the oils cool to the same temperature. When the temperatures match, pour the lye solution in a thin stream into the oils. Stir constantly until the mixture traces, about 10–20 minutes. (If you use an immersion blender, take care not to whip air into the mixture.)

5. When the soap batter traces, add the fragrance oil. (It will not turn the soap brown immediately.) Add the castor oil. Pour the batter into the mold, taking care to scrape all the traced soap out of the cup.

Cover the mold with plastic wrap. Place the mold on a towel and fold the extra over the mold to keep it warm. Cover this recipe very lightly, or not at all if the weather is warm. You want it to go through the gel phase, but you don't want it to get too hot. Let sit for 2 days, and then unmold.

6. Using a stainless steel knife, cut the soap log into bars. Place them on a brown paper bag to dry. Turn them daily to be sure they dry evenly. With milk soap, be sure to check for the smell of ammonia. It is normal to have a little bit of an ammonia smell, but if it doesn't go away in a week, it probably isn't going to.

7. In 4 weeks, your soap will be mild and quite firm and ready to use.

MOMMY AND ME

If you are nursing, you can make an incredible soap for your baby's skin. The lactic acid helps clear up rashes and helps keep skin soft. Making this soap for a nursing friend is a beautiful gift to her and her baby. Mommy and Daddy can use it too, of course.

➤ YIELDS APPROXIMATELY 24 OUNCES ◄

10 ounces olive oil

6 ounces coconut oil

6 ounces breast milk, frozen

2.25 ounces lye

¼ teaspoon lavender essential oil (optional)

¼ teaspoon Roman chamomile essential oil (optional)

1 tablespoon castor oil

1. Combine the olive oil and coconut oil in a heatproof glass 4-cup measure. Melt in the microwave or over boiling water. (Do not overheat, as it takes oils longer to cool than the lye solution. You will be combining the lye and oils at a very low temperature.)

2. Place the breast milk in a wide, deep tempered glass or stainless steel mixing bowl. (The idea is to keep the mixture shallow.) Break up the frozen chunks so the breast milk is slushy but not melted.

3. Sprinkle the lye *very* slowly and carefully over the slushy breast milk, stirring constantly. (As you stir, the mixture will become very pale yellow. If you add the lye too fast or don't stir as you go, you could end up with an overheated, brown, curdled mess.)

4. Check the temperature of the breast milk and lye solution. Let the oils cool to the same temperature. When the temperatures match, pour the lye solution in a thin stream into the oils. Stir constantly until the mixture traces, about 10–20 minutes. (If you use an immersion blender, take care not to whip air into the mixture.)

5. When the soap batter traces, add the lavender essential oil and chamomile essential oil, if you have decided to use them. Add the castor oil and stir well. Pour into the mold, taking care to scrape all the traced soap out of the cup.

6. Cover the mold with plastic wrap. Place the mold on a towel and fold the extra over the mold to keep it warm. (Cover this recipe very lightly, or not at all if the weather is warm. You want it to go through the gel phase, but you don't want it to get too hot.) Let sit for 2 days and then unmold.

7. Using a stainless steel knife, cut the soap log into bars. Place them on a brown paper bag to dry. Turn them daily to be sure they dry evenly. With milk soap, be sure to check for the smell of ammonia. It is normal to have a little bit of an ammonia smell, but if it doesn't go away in a week, it probably isn't going to.

8. In 4 weeks, your soap will be mild and quite firm and ready to use.

CAUTION WITH BABIES

Don't use soap on infants under six months old. When you decide to bathe your baby with your handmade soap, test a small area of skin first to be sure she is not irritated by it. Always check with your baby's pediatrician before trying something new.

EMBOSSING WITH STAMPS

Want to easily add an extra touch to your soap? Try embossing your soap with a stamp. Right after the bars are cut, the smooth, even surfaces are in perfect condition for these two simple and beautiful ways to embellish your creations.

Embossing

Even though we use tools called "stamps" when we leave an impression on a bar of soap, we are embossing it. To stamp would be to simply use the stamp to apply color.

You can add a design element with specially designed soap stamps, or certain rubber stamps and leather stamps, or you can easily make your own, personalized stamp using polymer clays. You need to do this step soon after cutting, depending on the hardness of the bar.

Besides the stamp impression—the embossing—itself, you can further embellish your soap design by dipping the stamp in mica or soap paint before placing it on the surface of the soap. Besides being decorative, it is very helpful in getting the stamp to release from soft, sticky soap. The design will wash away with use, but it doesn't take away from the initial impact of a further realization of your creativity. Some stamps allow you to leave just mica on the surface, with no embossed indentation. You can also use stamps to enhance your soap-casting creations, making them even more beautiful.

Soap Stamps

It is possible to find rubber stamps and leather stamps that will work for embossing soap. You want to look for designs that are simple and have bold lines. The depth of the stamp is important, too. It needs to be able to penetrate the surface of the soap enough to leave an impression. When using metal stamps, the soap must be neutral, of course, and as with all stamps, you need to clean the stamp of soap residue as it may eventually decay the stamp and shorten its useful life.

You can get customized stamps in a number of ways. Soap Impressions is a small company that will create a soap stamp from your own art. They also have premade letter sets and a few designs.

Making Stamps with Polymer Clay

Making your own custom stamp is easier than you probably think. You make a "negative" mold and use that to make the stamp from hard-baking polymer clay. You can create a built-in handle or glue the stamp shape onto a wooden handle. You take that shape and use it to stamp your soap. If you've worked with polymer clay, you have probably used molds called "push molds," and this is a custom version of that kind of mold.

Making the negative is essentially the same as making the soap mold from Chapter 3. The main difference between making a mold for soap and making a mold to make a stamp is that with a stamp you want the impression to be shallow, whereas for a soap mold you want the impression to be deep. For your stamp, choose an object that is shallow and of a size that will fit well on the surface of your soap bars. Here's what you need to make the stamp:

- Flexible mold-making polymer clay
- Water spray
- Small decorative object to make into a mold, such as an earring, pendant, shell, or stone
- Foil
- Baking sheet
- Polymer clay
- Medium-grit sandpaper
- Epoxy
- Small block of wood

Each brand of polymer clay is different. Where directions differ between these directions and those that came with the clay, follow the directions for the variety of polymer clay you choose.

Decide on the image you want to stamp onto your soap. As with so many things in soapmaking, your choices are virtually endless. For a place to start, think in terms of themes. Seasons, events, holidays, and hobbies hold many ideas for images.

Objects with a shallow depth—approximately ⅛"—are ideal. If you use objects that make too deep an imprint, the stamp will displace too much soap and distort the bar and the image.

Before you start, prepare your workspace, gather all the materials, and preheat the oven to the temperature designated in the instructions for the clay you are using.

1. Work the flexible polymer clay with your hands to make it pliable. Make a tablet shape: flat on the bottom and on the top with a large enough surface area for the design, and deep enough to take the full impression.
2. Lightly spritz the surface of the object with water and wipe off drips. (The fine coating of water will help release the object from the clay.)
3. Push the object into the clay and remove it quickly. If the impression is good, use it. If the impression is unclear, re-form the tablet and try again. The clay will get softer and warmer the more you work it with your hands, so let it cool for better results. You can use one tablet for a few small impressions, if you like. When using multiple items on one tablet, be sure to allow room for the clay to move and spread between images without distortion.
4. Place the foil on the baking sheet, and put the mold on the foil. Bake the flexible mold clay as directed on the package (generally, at 275°F for 10 minutes per ¼" of thickness). When baked, cool on a heatproof surface.

5. Once the master mold is cool, you can make your stamp. Work the regular polymer clay to condition it. Spray the mold with a fine mist of water—the film of water and the flexible nature of the mold-making polymer clay will make it quite easy to remove the shape. Push it into the mold, making sure to get the clay into each detail. You can make a handle for the stamp by pushing more clay into the mold than is needed to fill it. Work the extra into a little handle shape.

6. Flex the mold and gently work out the shape.

7. Bake the shapes as directed (generally, at 275°F for 10 minutes per ¼" of thickness).

8. After baking, remove the shapes and let them cool. If needed, smooth rough edges, and smooth the flat back with medium-grit sandpaper if you're going to attach it to a wooden handle. You may have better success in stamping soft soap if you make a handle as part of the shape.

9. Use epoxy to affix the stamp shape to a small piece of wood to use as a handle. If you stamp soap when it's hard, you may need to be able to hit it with a mallet, so make sure the handle you choose will stand up to it.

For a beautiful decorative touch, before you use the stamp on your soap, dip the stamp in mica, tap off any excess, and press the stamp into the soap. It will leave both the impression and a sparkle.

Polymer clay stamps will adhere to or release from your soap depending on the formula, the age of the soap, and other factors including humidity and temperature in the work space. If your stamp isn't releasing easily, you may need to brush the stamp with oil, nonstick cooking spray, or a silicone release agent such as cyclomethicone. Do what works.

CHAPTER FIVE

HOT-PROCESS SOAPMAKING

Now that you've got the hang of cold-process soapmaking, let's move on to hot process. This is basically an extension of the cold-process technique. The still-caustic soap batter is cooked for several hours, forcing it to neutralize. One major benefit is that the soap is ready for immediate use! Another is that you can add precious essential oils in very small amounts and get all their benefits. In this chapter you'll learn how to make hot-process soaps, and you'll find a number of possible recipes for them.

UNDERSTANDING HOT PROCESS

The primary reason for making hot-process soap is that you can use it right away. Unlike cold-process soap, you don't have to wait for hot-process soap to cure. The "hot" part of the processing is cooking the soap over low heat until it neutralizes. This is a timesaver over cold-process soapmaking because in cold process you have to wait for the soap to neutralize on its own.

Is It Neutral Yet?

You can usually use hot-process soap as soon as it cools. Have phenolphthalein or litmus strips on hand to check the soap's pH. If you use litmus paper, follow the directions on the package. Litmus paper is not the best method for testing soap; the results are not always accurate, and it is difficult to read. If you use phenolphthalein, the pH test is very simple: Put a few drops on the soap. If it turns pink, the soap is still alkaline. If the soap is neutral, the drops will stay clear. Test the soap when it is still in the slow cooker. If it is alkaline, cook it longer.

Molding and Unmolding

You can use individual bar molds for hot-process soap. Since the soap at time of "pour" is very thick, you need to be sure to cram the soap into the details of intricate molds. You will have better luck with individual molds if you use oils that produce harder bars, just as in cold process. Don't forget beeswax when making a recipe for individual molds!

You unmold and cut it the same way as you do in cold process. You will usually have to trim the top surface, since it is nearly impossible to get the top smooth, due to the clumpy nature of hot-process soap at time of pour. The longer you wait for the water to evaporate from the bars, the harder the soap will be.

Color and Scent Additives

Color and scent materials are added after "the cook." You can use less essential oil this way, since it is not exposed to the batter when it is still caustic. Stirring in the additives can be difficult at this stage because the soap is very thick and gloppy, but it can be done without an enormous amount of energy.

You'll stir in fragrance and other things that need complete dispersion first. Then, if you're going to swirl or marble, you'll need to separate out the amounts of soap you're going to color. You'll tint each part individually and then mix them together. The effect will be different from the fluid swirls of cold process, but the effects are beautiful.

If you're going to color the batch all the same color, you can do it at the beginning; if you're using colorants that are not affected by lye, such as ultramarines, you can add them at an earlier stage than in cold-process soapmaking. With any lye soap batch, you can add ultramarines to the lye solution to ensure complete blending of color.

Remember when using any kind of colorant that the best way to know how to get exactly the color you want is experience. In hot-process soapmaking, you can add colors that didn't perform well with cold process and usually get a better result. Know that there is no way to know exactly how it will look until you try.

Soap Texture

There is a difference in the texture of hot- and cold-processed soap. Cold process tends to have a finer, firmer texture, while hot process can be more coarse and a little spongy. However, with practice, you can make hot-process soap with nearly the same exquisite texture as cold process.

The texture problems of hot-process soap comes from evaporation, or lack of it. The amount of water used at the start is the same as in the cold-process recipe. If too much water evaporates during the cook, the soap can be grainy. If not enough evaporates, or if you use too much at the start, the soap can be spongy.

As long as the soap is neutral, graininess and sponginess are merely aesthetic issues. Another common result of too much water is bars that warp as they age. A good use for soap that is unattractive but otherwise completely fine is to use it for chunks in cold process, or grated for hand-milling projects.

Cooking to Neutrality

There are many ways to cook the soap to neutrality. The easiest way is to cook the caustic batter in a slow cooker. The slow cooker hot-process method is gaining popularity over the common double-boiler method. The major drawback for many soapmakers is that there are more size limits on slow cookers than on stock pots. Some soapers take the stainless steel pot of traced soap and put it in the oven to do the cook.

There are soapmaking message boards dedicated to advanced techniques in hot-process soapmaking. You can find soapers who place their molds in the sun, on hot driveways, and in plastic bags inside the double boiler. Once you've gained experience with the basic methods, find a group of soapers who've come up with further specialized techniques, and experiment.

HOT-PROCESS EQUIPMENT

In addition to the equipment needed for cold-process soapmaking, the hot-process technique requires either a slow cooker or a double boiler.

Slow Cooker

The recipes in this book call for a slow cooker. They are easy to use, self-contained, and convenient. You can purchase slow cookers at mass market, outlet, overstock, and thrift stores, ranging in size from mini to great big 8-quart slow cookers. The recipes in the book call for a 3½-quart slow cooker. If you want to increase the size of your recipe, get a bigger slow cooker. Just make sure you have enough headroom to accommodate the puffing up that will often happen. An overflowing mass of caustic soap is a surprise you don't want.

Calculate the volume of your batch—oils plus water plus lye—and fill the crock with that much water. There should be at least 2" of free space left from the top of the slow cooker to the surface.

Double Boiler

Instead of a slow cooker, you can cook your hot-process soap in a double boiler made from two large pots, one placed inside the other. Depending on the size of your recipe, you can use something as large as a canning kettle with a 12-quart stock pot inside, down to one small saucepan placed inside another.

The type of commercial "sit on top" double boiler you buy in stores is not the ideal pan for small batches of hot-process cooking. The airspace at the top stays cooler than you need for an efficient cook. It's better to have the soap pot partially submerged in the boiling water of the bigger pan.

Kitchen supply stores usually carry a trivet-like object for "making" a double boiler. You place it in the bottom of the larger pot and sit the smaller pot on top of it. You can, of course, use other common kitchen items, such as metal lids or canning jar rings, to lift the smaller pot off the bottom of the bigger one.

Getting Started

You can use just about any cold-process recipe to make an opaque hot-process batch. (This is not true, though, for liquid and transparent hot-process recipes, which require different ingredients.) It is a good idea to make the recipe as a cold-process batch first to know what to expect.

Although cold process takes weeks to neutralize, waiting can be less stressful for beginners than cooking the soap to neutrality. Know that, like any new recipe and technique, hot-process soapmaking will become routine for you.

The following basic hot-process recipe is the same as the basic cold-process recipe. However, the convenience that you find with a 1-pound batch in cold-process soapmaking isn't that convenient with hot process. It's easier to get the cook going with a bigger batch, but too large a batch can be quite unwieldy. The recipes here are a compromise—not too small, not too large.

BASIC HOT-PROCESS SOAP

❧ YIELDS 3 POUNDS ❧

1.33 pounds olive oil
3 ounces palm kernel oil
10 ounces coconut oil
12 ounces water
4.5 ounces lye
2 tablespoons castor oil
Your choice of scent materials
Your choice of color
Your choice of other additives

1. Combine and melt the olive oil, palm kernel oil, and coconut oil in the slow cooker.

2. Place the water in a heatproof container. Slowly add the lye to prepare the lye solution. Heat the oils and cool the lye solution until both are 110°F. Pour the lye solution into the oils, slowly and carefully. Stir to trace. Add the castor oil.

3. Cook in the slow cooker, 3 hours on low setting. Check for consistency every 30 minutes. Check pH. Add the scent materials, color, and other additives when neutral.

4. Pack into molds, let cool, and set. Unmold, cut into bars, and store as usual.

COFFEE KITCHEN SOAP

It is common soapmaking lore that ground coffee has a deodorizing effect on the skin. Coffee is said to be able to remove the odors of garlic and onions from your hands. You'll have to see for yourself.

❧ YIELDS 3 POUNDS ❧

2-pound batch recipe of your choice, substituting strong brewed coffee for the water
2 tablespoons finely ground coffee

1. Make up the batch as usual and stir to a good medium trace.

2. Cook as usual. Check pH. Continue cooking if it's still caustic, until the soap is neutral.

3. Stir the finely ground coffee into the neutral soap.

4. Pack into molds, let cool, and set. Unmold, cut into bars, and store as usual.

LEMON–BAKING SODA KITCHEN SOAP

Lemons have long been prized for their ability to reduce kitchen odors, as has baking soda. Baking soda is also a gentle abrasive. Lemon zest helps cut grease and adds a fresh lemon scent.

➤ YIELDS 3 POUNDS ◄

2-pound batch recipe of your choice

2 tablespoons lemon zest

3 tablespoons baking soda

1. Make up the batch as usual and stir to a good medium trace.

2. Cook as usual until the soap is neutral. Check pH. Continue cooking if it's still caustic, and check again.

3. Stir the lemon zest and baking soda into the neutral soap.

4. Pack into molds, let cool, and set. Unmold, cut into bars, and store as usual.

SUPER-CLEAN KITCHEN SOAP

Orange, eucalyptus, and lavender essential oils are great grease cutters. These essential oils are also known for their reported antibacterial properties. Cornmeal adds brisk abrasive action.

➤ YIELDS 3 POUNDS ◄

2-pound batch recipe of your choice
2 tablespoons yellow cornmeal
½ teaspoon orange essential oil
½ teaspoon eucalyptus essential oil
½ teaspoon lavender essential oil

1. Make up the batch as usual and stir to a good medium trace.

2. Cook as usual until the soap is neutral. Check pH. Continue cooking if it's still caustic, and check again.

3. Stir the yellow cornmeal into the neutral soap. Add the orange essential oil, eucalyptus essential oil, and lavender essential oil. Stir well.

4. Pack into molds, let cool, and set. Unmold, cut into bars, and store as usual.

PEPPERMINT BATH SOAP

Every tub should have at least one good bath soap. Single essential oils can make for an easy choice in the morning. Choose peppermint for a brisk awakening.

➤ YIELDS 3 POUNDS ◄

2-pound batch recipe of your choice, substituting strong mint tea—made from fresh peppermint, mint tea bags, or loose tea, strained well and cooled—for the water
1 tablespoon mint, dried and ground (you can use the contents of a mint tea bag)
½ teaspoon peppermint essential oil

1. Make up the batch as usual and stir to a good medium trace.

2. Cook as usual until the soap is neutral. Check pH. Continue cooking if it's still caustic.

3. Stir the mint into the neutral soap. Just before you pack the soap into the molds, add the peppermint essential oil. (Wait as long as possible to stir in the essential oil. It is extremely volatile—readily vaporized—and your house will smell like an explosion in a toothpaste factory.)

4. Pack into molds, let cool, and set. Unmold, cut into bars, and store as usual.

LAVENDER BATH SOAP

To make the lavender infusion called for in this recipe, use 2 tablespoons of lavender for each cup of water in the recipe. Heat the water and pour it over the lavender. Let cool and then strain out the lavender. Remeasure. Add more water to compensate for any volume that may have been lost due to evaporation.

➤ **YIELDS 3 POUNDS** ◄

2-pound batch recipe of your choice, substituting a lavender infusion for the water
1 tablespoon dried lavender flowers
1 teaspoon lavender essential oil

1. Make up the batch as usual and stir to a good medium trace.
2. Cook as usual until the soap is neutral. Check pH. Continue cooking if it's still caustic.
3. Stir the lavender flowers into the neutral soap. Add the lavender essential oil and stir completely.
4. Pack into molds, let cool, and set. Unmold, cut into bars, and store as usual.

ROSEMARY BATH SOAP

Rosemary is great for mental focus. To make the rosemary infusion called for in this recipe, use 2 tablespoons of rosemary for each cup of water in the recipe. Heat the water and pour it over the rosemary. Let cool and then strain out the rosemary. Remeasure. Add more water to compensate for any volume that may have been lost due to evaporation.

➤ **YIELDS 3 POUNDS** ◄

2-pound batch recipe of your choice, substituting a rosemary infusion for the water
1 tablespoon finely chopped rosemary leaves
1 teaspoon rosemary essential oil

1. Make up the batch as usual and stir to a good medium trace.
2. Cook as usual until the soap is neutral. Check pH. Continue cooking if it's still caustic.
3. Stir the rosemary leaves into the neutral soap. Add the rosemary essential oil and stir completely.
4. Pack into molds, let cool, and set. Unmold, cut into bars, and store as usual.

Perfect Facial Soap

Contrary to common understanding, soap and water are good for almost any face. It just has to be the right soap. Properly formulated handmade soap makes a great facial soap. Whether your skin is dry, average, oily, or prone to breakouts, there is a good chance handmade facial soap will work for you.

The following recipes make small batches, as you'll be using more costly ingredients. You can, of course, make these recipes using the cold-process technique, but with hot process, you can use less of the costly essential oils. Cool the soap as much as you can before stirring in the essential oils. This way you'll have less evaporation of the precious oils.

SOAP FOR DRY SKIN

5 ounces olive oil

5 ounces coconut oil

3 ounces shea butter

3 ounces avocado oil

6 ounces water

1 tablespoon dried chamomile

2.25 ounces lye

0.5 ounce castor oil

10 drops German chamomile essential oil

5 drops rose otto essential oil

2 drops jasmine essential oil

5 drops palmarosa essential oil

1. Combine and melt the olive oil, coconut oil, shea butter, and avocado oil in the slow cooker.

2. Make a chamomile infusion by heating the water and pouring it over the chamomile. Let cool, then strain out the chamomile. Remeasure. Add more water to make 6 ounces, to compensate for evaporation.

3. Place the chamomile infusion in a heatproof container. Slowly add the lye to prepare the lye solution. Heat the oils and cool the lye solution until both are 110°F. Pour the lye solution into the oils, slowly and carefully. Stir to trace. Add the castor oil.

4. Cook in the slow cooker, 3 hours on low setting. Check for consistency every 30 minutes. Check pH.

5. When the soap is neutral, add the chamomile essential oil, rose otto essential oil, jasmine essential oil, and palmarosa essential oil and stir thoroughly.

6. Pack into molds, let cool, and set. Unmold, cut into bars, and store as usual.

SOAP FOR SKIN THAT'S NOT TOO OILY OR TOO DRY

8 ounces olive oil

4 ounces coconut oil

4 ounces macadamia nut oil

6 ounces water

1 tablespoon dried lavender

2.25 ounces lye

0.5 ounce castor oil

5 drops German chamomile
    essential oil

2 drops rose otto essential oil

⅛ teaspoon lavender essential
    oil

1. Combine and melt the olive oil, coconut oil, and macadamia nut oil in the slow cooker.

2. Make a lavender infusion by heating the water and pouring it over the lavender. Let cool, then strain out the lavender. Remeasure. Add more water to make 6 ounces, to compensate for any volume that may have been lost due to evaporation.

3. Place the lavender infusion in a heatproof container. Slowly add the lye to prepare the lye solution. Heat the oils and cool the lye solution until both are 110°F. Pour the lye solution into the oils, slowly and carefully. Stir to trace. Add the castor oil.

4. Cook in the slow cooker, 3 hours on low setting. Check for consistency every 30 minutes. Check pH.

5. When the soap is neutral, add the chamomile essential oil, rose otto essential oil, and lavender essential oil and stir thoroughly.

6. Pack into molds, let cool, and set. Unmold, cut into bars, and store as usual.

SOAP FOR OILY SKIN

6 ounces olive oil

4 ounces coconut oil

6 ounces grapeseed oil

6 ounces strong-brewed
   black tea

2.25 ounces lye

0.5 ounce castor oil

¼ teaspoon lavender
   essential oil

5 drops cedarwood
   essential oil

5 drops lemongrass
   essential oil

5 drops rosemary
   essential oil

1. Combine and melt the olive oil, coconut oil, and grapeseed oil in the slow cooker.

2. Place the tea in a heatproof container. Slowly add the lye to prepare the lye solution. Heat the oils and cool the lye solution until both are 110°F. Pour the lye solution into the oils, slowly and carefully. Stir to trace. Add the castor oil.

3. Cook in the slow cooker, 3 hours on low setting. Check for consistency every 30 minutes. Check pH.

4. When the soap is neutral, add the lavender essential oil, cedarwood essential oil, lemongrass essential oil, and rosemary essential oil and stir thoroughly.

5. Pack into molds, let cool, and set. Unmold, cut into bars, and store as usual.

SOAP FOR ACNE-PRONE SKIN

11 ounces olive oil

5 ounces coconut oil

6 ounces water

1 tablespoon hibiscus tea blend

2.25 ounces lye

1 tablespoon bentonite or kaolin clay

0.5 ounce castor oil

6 drops tea tree essential oil

6 drops lavender essential oil

6 drops rosemary essential oil

1. Combine and melt the olive oil and coconut oil in the slow cooker.

2. Make a hibiscus tea by heating the water and pouring it over the hibiscus tea blend. Let cool and then strain out the hibiscus. Remeasure. Add more water to make 6 ounces, to compensate for any volume that may have been lost due to evaporation.

3. Place the tea in a heatproof container. Slowly add the lye and the clay to prepare the lye solution. Heat the oils and cool the lye solution until both are 110°F. Pour the lye solution into the oils, slowly and carefully. Stir to trace. Add the castor oil.

4. Cook in the slow cooker, 3 hours on low setting. Check for consistency every 30 minutes. Check pH.

5. When the soap is neutral, add the tea tree essential oil, lavender essential oil, and rosemary essential oil and stir thoroughly.

6. Pack into molds, let cool, and set. Unmold, cut into bars, and store as usual.

Unmolding

Getting hot-process soaps out of their molds can be a challenge. You'll have to use trial and error. Some batches are just stickier than others. Some may release with no trouble at all, and others may take extended time in the molds before they'll release.

CREATING COLOR VARIATION

Creating color variation in hot-process soap can be tricky. But it can be done. It takes a bit of planning and coordination, but you can do it easily once you've got the knack. Think of each color as a "sub-batch," each with its own mixing vessel. Your most useful tools are a stainless steel slotted spoon, a small whisk, and a scoop-shaped silicone spatula. Use your heat-resistant glass bowls and measures to blend the individual colors. You will also find stainless steel soupspoons and wooden chopsticks helpful.

Experiment with Patterns

Make up the batch and cook to neutrality. While it is cooking, set up the colorants, fragrances, and mixing cups. If the colors and scents vary widely, have separate stirring spoons for each sub-batch.

RIBBONS OF COLOR

You can make long strips of color by packing the different colors side by side in ribbons. If you want a pastry-like effect, you'll then drag a chopstick widthwise through the ribbons. Each batch will, of course, be unique. Stay open to the marvelous variation and unplanned beauty.

Plan out the pattern you want to attempt. If you want large chunks of color, you'll place blobs of colored soap in the mold in the color pattern you like, and leave it. If you want to swirl, you can push a chopstick through those blobs in various directions, depending on the effect you want.

Glopping and Swirling

Although it sounds inelegant, "glop" is an apt verb for describing the way you make color variations in hot process. The hot-process soap is thick, so you won't be able to get the subtle swirls you get with the fluidity of cold-process swirling. You can, however, create great-looking soap.

Divide the hot, neutralized soap into as many containers as you have colors. You must work quickly: The cooler the soap gets, the more difficult it will be to incorporate the color evenly. As with other coloring techniques, removing a bit of soap, coloring it, and then stirring that back into the rest works best. Once you've incorporated the colors, you're going to glop them into the mold. You will place each portion in a certain way to get the effect you want. The soap will be solid enough to support the portion you place on top of it.

You can make an orderly pattern with the portions of colored soap. Try stripes of one color one way across the mold, and another set of stripes of a different color going the other way.

To make swirls, run a chopstick, spoon, or narrow spatula through the layers. Go randomly or in a pattern, whatever you think will look good. Be sure to make the swirls evenly from the bottom to the top of the mold. It's easy to miss the bottom of the mold.

SCULPTING WITH HOT-PROCESS SOAP

This is another technique that is to be undertaken only by an experienced soapmaker. You must have command of the hot process and be confident that you know for certain when it is neutral. If you have any doubts, then do not use this technique. And although there is a major element of play involved, this is not a technique for beginners.

One of the challenges of hot-process soap is how to form it. Finding just the right temperature and consistency to achieve the shape and texture you want may lead you to work with still-warm soap, right from the slow cooker. When the soap is cool enough to handle, knead it and work it until it is smooth, and then roll it into soap balls. Play around with other shapes; the soap will be pliable for quite some time before becoming too firm to work. Ovals, little cubes, then figures will emerge as you realize that warm, neutral, fresh hot-processed soap is an apt material for sculpture.

As the warm—even hot—soap is worked by hand, it takes on a lovely smoothness that looks and feels good in simple shapes, for example spheres, cubes, and eggs. You can work more complicated shapes: human and animal forms, logs you can make into knots, abstracts—anything that emerges as you work.

At the end of your sculpting session, you'll have an array of shapes, objects, and figures. And the feeling in your hands is incredible—the deep heat combined with the kneading is the most amazing hand massage you've ever had. Your hands may be dry after working with soap for such an extended time, so be sure to apply a rich hand lotion or cream after you've enjoyed the lather of your new soap.

Sculpting Project

Make the batch of hot-process soap of your choice. When the soap is almost done, gather the following tools:

- 1 batch hot-process soap

- Newspaper, kraft paper, or cardboard

- Waxed paper

- Large serving spoon

- Scale (optional)

- Bowl of ice water to quickly cool your hands if needed

- Some additions and decorations, such as dried herbs and flower petals, coffee beans, dried white beans, large tapioca, or smooth stones to put in the center of the soap to find like treasure as the soap washes away. (Remember that this list is just the beginning of what you can use—feel free to get creative!)

- Bamboo skewers or stainless steel or plastic spoons, forks, and knives

1. Test the hot-process for neutrality. *You must not skip this step. You must be absolutely certain the soap is completely neutral.* Turn off the heat of the slow cooker or stove.

2. Cover your work surface with the newspaper, kraft paper, or cardboard.

3. Cut about 10 placemat-sized pieces of waxed paper. (You'll use these as a direct work surface, and they wear out, so cut more than you think you'll need.)

4. Scoop out a portion of soap onto a piece of waxed paper. If you want to be precise about the size of the soaps, place the waxed paper on the scale and weigh out the amount of soap you want. Four ounces is a good starting place. If you don't want to weigh it, you can judge by eye a scoop about as big as a stick of butter.

5. To facilitate cooling, smash and spread the scoop of hot soap until it's about ¼" thick. The soap will stay molten inside even when the outside looks dry and cool, so keep smashing it with the spoon until it's warm, but not too hot.

6. Carefully test the soap for temperature by touching it. You need to be sure it's cool enough not to burn you, yet warm enough to work. If you're uncertain, start with an ounce or so, and familiarize yourself with how it cools.

7. When you have a mass of soap that is cool enough to work, flatten it with your hands. Roll it and knead it and shape it. You'll observe that it goes from coarse texture to smooth as you work it. When it starts to get too cool to work, it will become almost waxy feeling, and sometimes crumble if you continue to work it. If you're adding herbs, for example, sprinkle crushed dried herbs onto the flattened mass, and then knead them into it by smashing and rolling, pushing and squishing. If at any time it feels uncomfortably hot, put it down and smash it with the spoon to thin it out so it can cool more.

8. When the soap is smooth, shape it the way you want it, using bamboo skewers or stainless steel or plastic spoons, forks, and knives. Blocks, spheres, and pyramids are great starter shapes and will be able to take an imprint from a soap stamp, rubber stamp, or other embossing tool.

As you gain facility with simple shapes, others will emerge. If you find yourself getting frustrated, try to stop thinking and just let your mind and hands work together. The sculpted shapes may look rough at first, but they will smooth when you wash with them. Like with all handmade soap, be sure to set your soap sculptures on a soap dish or other well-drained place to keep it from dissolving.

CLEANING UP

Whatever you do, don't rinse large blobs of gooey soap, either finished or unsaponified, down your drains. They will clog up your drains almost immediately and take a lot to clean out once clogged.

When making hot-process soap, do your cleanup in stages. While the soap is cooking, clean up the tools and equipment that were touched by lye and raw soap. Always wear gloves and goggles when cleaning up after working with lye.

Wipe excess soap off the tools, and then put them in the sink with a generous amount of white vinegar. Use about ½–1 cup per sink load. Add detergent and wash well, followed with another rinse of hot water. If the tools and equipment still feel oily, wash again with detergent and hot water.

After your hot-process soap is done, it is neutral, so you may continue your cleanup without so many safety precautions. Still take care. Don't rinse chunks down the drain, and make sure there is no greasy residue.

LEMONIZE!

Lemons can be a great help in cleaning up after a round of oily soaping. Cut the lemons in half and keep them close by so you can squeeze the juice on your skin after you've rinsed away a lye splash with water, and add lemon juice to your wash water. Lemon essential oil is also a great degreaser.

CHAPTER SIX

HERBS YOU CAN PUT IN YOUR SOAP

Now that you know the basics of the two methods of soapmaking and, possibly, have tried one or two of the recipes in the previous chapters, it's time to step up your game.

One of the most creative and fun aspects of soapmaking is deciding what to put in your soap. After all, this is where you craft your bars to meet your own tastes—or those of the people to whom you're planning to gift the soaps. The online soapmaking community can give you a lot of tips, but in this chapter and the following one we'll cover some of the most common ingredients in artisanal soaps.

One of the most common ingredients of artisanal soaps is herbs. That's because herbs are natural—you can grow them in your back garden or on a pot on your kitchen windowsill—and versatile. You can use fresh or dried herbs in soapmaking, keeping in mind that the flavor and aroma of dried herbs is more concentrated and intense than in the fresh version. In general, as explained in the following sections, dried herbs are preferable.

USING HERBS IN SOAPMAKING

In soap, herbs add color and texture. Many soapmakers also believe that the medicinal value of herbs can come through in soaps made with them. As with other natural substances, not all herbs are beneficial to humans. There are poisonous herbs that you should avoid. Some herbs, while not toxic, are dermal irritants and should not be used on the skin. Take special care when using herbs with children, the elderly, and people with special healthcare needs. Make sure to do your research, and be responsible and informed when deciding what to use in your soaps.

Adding Herbs to Soap

The most obvious way to add herbs to soap is to sprinkle them in the soap before you pour it into the mold. An addition of a small amount of a dried herb creates a delicate visual texture. Adding a larger amount of a roughly chopped fresh herb can lend a "scrubby" texture to the soap. In general, it is best to use dried herbs, as the water in fresh herbs can, among other problems, cause mold to grow.

Adding Herbs to Water

Replacing the water in your soap recipe with an herbal infusion is another simple way to add herbs to soap. Make the infusion and strain out the solid matter, if you wish, before making the lye solution. The infusion may take on a strange color and odor when the lye is added, but that will usually fade away completely in the finished soap.

KNOW YOUR INGREDIENTS

Be sure that all herbs you use are nontoxic. If you are in doubt, put aside the questionable herb and use something you're sure about. Also, if you are pregnant, nursing, have diabetes or other health issues, be sure to consult your healthcare provider about the use of herbs. Herbs are active substances that may react with medical conditions or medications.

Another way to use herbs in soap is to make a lye infusion. To do this, add ground herbs to the water as you add the lye. The extremely rapid reaction of lye and water can release more of the properties of the herb than the relatively gentle method of making an herbal infusion. It is most likely that a great deal of the benefit of the herb will be destroyed in the reaction, but some herbs release more lasting color when added in this manner.

Herbs in Oil

Infusing liquid oils with herbs is yet another way of extracting their properties for use in soap. Making infused oils for soapmaking is easy. First warm the oil (the most common liquid soapmaking oil is olive oil) and place the plant matter in the heated oil. Then let the herbs steep in the heated oil for a number of hours or even days, depending on the herb and the strength of the infusion you desire. You can increase the potency by straining out the herbs, rewarming the oil, and adding more herbs. Some oils can be tinted deeply in this manner so that the natural colorant survives the soapmaking process.

Herbs in Soap Processes

In soap casting, you can add herbs in such a way that they sink to the bottom, float on the top, or are suspended throughout the bar. Through control of temperature, you can achieve whichever effect you desire. You can also add small amounts of herbal-infused water or oils to the soap base.

The soapmaking method that may retain most of the herbal properties is hand milling. You can take shreds of premade cold-process or casting soap, toss them with herbs, sprinkle the mixture with herbal infusion, and create balls or other shapes by hand.

In hot process, you can add the herbs right before you pack the soap into the molds, when the soap is coolest and has the least impact on the herbs. You can stir them in or you can knead the herbs in by hand, wearing thick rubber gloves to protect your hands from the hot soap.

GROWING YOUR OWN HERBS

Many herbs are very easy to grow, and drying and using them will contribute to the artisanal nature of your soaps. Soapmaking favorites such as lavender, calendula, and peppermint can easily be grown in small containers in a window. If you have a garden, the addition of even a small number of herbs for soap greatly enriches your soapmaking. Some soapers have herb gardens dedicated just to soap herbs.

If you are an avid gardener, there is virtually no limit to the kinds of herbs you can grow. If you are limited by time, inexperience, or other factors, select just a few. The herbs that follow are very useful in soapmaking and generally very easy to grow.

Calendula

Calendula grows best in full sun in well-drained soil. It is vigorous and a beautiful addition to your garden. It is, however, susceptible to a plant disease called powdery mildew, so keep an eye on it. You can make a good anti–powdery mildew spray out of grated soap dissolved in water with borax powder added to it.

Comfrey

Comfrey is a vigorous grower that will take over your garden if given a chance. Keep it confined to a pot or give it a corner of its own where it can run wild. Harvest and dry the leaves as you trim the vigorously growing plant.

Lavender

Lavender brings fragrance and beauty to all gardens and can readily transmit that to your artisanal soap. There are so many kinds of lavenders, you can find one that goes with any gardening style. Munstead lavender is a small plant, and it is extremely fragrant. The little flowers grow outside on the heads and are easily used for sachets, after drying.

Lavender needs rich, well-drained soil. Don't let its roots stay wet! An addition of sand and calcium-rich nutrients to the soil makes lavender plants very happy.

Mint

Peppermint and spearmint are easy to grow, and like comfrey, will take over your garden. They send out runners, so keep them corralled in pots or give them room. Trim plants back frequently to encourage bushy growth, and dry the leaves.

Rosemary

Rosemary thrives in cooler climates. Prostrate rosemary has soft stems and grows in a beautiful trailing form. The leaves are needle-like and can be very "poky" in soap, so be sure to finely chop the dried leaves.

DRYING AND STORING HERBS

Whether you harvest herbs from your garden or use fresh herbs from the store, you need to dry them prior to use. The water in fresh herbs can spoil your soap. You can dry herbs in the microwave, by hanging them in bundles in an airy room, or by spreading them out in a single layer on a flat surface. Hanging them or drying them on a flat surface is the most natural way to do this and will also fill your house with their lovely smell.

Bundling

If you have a shady window, you can dry herbs there. Bundle the herbs in small bunches and tie them with raffia, string, yarn, or embroidery thread in colorful combinations for a pretty touch. Don't bundle them too tightly because that prevents air circulation and can promote mold growth. Suspend the herb bundles from the curtain rod or from pins hammered into the wall or woodwork.

CHOOSE SHADE

It is best to dry herbs in a shady window because exposure to direct sunlight is thought to destroy the properties you're trying to preserve through air-drying. The reason you hang the herbs in a window is because of the air circulation. You want a balance of indirect light and air.

Check the herbs every day for a week or so. If they weren't bundled too tightly or too damp to start with and they get air circulation, they should be dry in 1 to 2 weeks. When the herbs are dry, store them in tightly sealed containers out of direct sunlight.

Laying Them Flat

You can speed up the drying process and keep most of the herbal properties intact by drying herbs on a cookie sheet on top of the stove. If you have a gas oven, the heat from the pilot light is enough to dry the herbs in a few days. If your range is electric, heat the oven to 200°F, turn it off, and put the cookie sheet of herbs on the top of the stove. Heat up the stove once a day.

COMMON SOAPMAKING HERBS

Although it can be a challenge to make sure the qualities of your herbs survive the soapmaking process, I strongly recommend you try to use them. Working with herbs is a real way to get "back to nature." As well, herbs are useful because of their color and texture possibilities, emphasizing the rustic nature of your homemade soap.

Here are some of the herbs used in soapmaking. If there is something you want to try that isn't on the list, go find out about it. If you are entranced by herbs, you have all kinds of resources available to you. You may even want to start your education by organizing your kitchen herb cupboard!

- **Aloe (*Aloe vera*).** Good for healing burns; available as fresh gel from aloe leaves, packaged gel, and in liquid form. Add fresh gel to casting soap and hand-milling projects just before pouring, or use aloe juice in place of water in lye soap recipes for skin care benefit.

- **Borage (*Borago officinalis*).** Anti-inflammatory and emollient; available as fresh or dried leaves and flowers. Take care with fresh leaves as they are very spiny. Infuse leaves and flowers in water or oil for skin care benefit.

- **Calendula (*Calendula officinalis*).** The herb is very susceptible to insect infestation, so store it in a tightly sealed plastic storage container. To make a healing oil, macerate fresh flowers in vegetable oil. Replenish the petals daily to concentrate the oil. Use in small amounts in hand milling and at the end of the hot process to add skin care benefit. The dried petals keep their shape in soapmaking.

- **Chamomile (*Chamaemelum nobile*, *Matricaria recutita*).** Has soothing, calming, and healing properties; available as fresh or dried flowers. Infuse in oil or water for herbal benefit. Use ground flowers to add texture and scrub benefit to finished soap. If used in quantity, the flowers hold some of their scent in some soapmaking applications.

- **Dandelion (*Taraxacum officinale*).** This common weed has healing and astringent properties. Don't use if the plants have been poisoned with weed killer. Make an infusion of leaves in water or oil for herbal benefit.

- **Dill (*Anethum graveolens*).** Has a tangy, fresh scent; available dried or as a fresh herb in the produce section. Dried dill holds its color quite well in soapmaking, even in cold process.

- **Lavender (*Lavandula augustifolia*).** Has soothing, calming, healing, and cleansing properties; available as dried flowering tops and leaves. Infuse water and oils for herbal benefit, but neither the color nor the fragrance makes it through the lye process well, if at all.

- **Lemon balm (*Melissa officinalis*).** Scent is deeply lemony, with varying degrees of mintiness; available as fresh or dried leaves. Oil and water infusions keep some scent through the lye soap process, but not much. Dried crumbled leaves add texture to finished soap.

- **Lemon verbena (*Aloysia triphylla*).** A lemony astringent; available as fresh or dried leaves. Use dried leaves in flakes or ground for texture in finished soap. Pick out stiff leaf parts and remember that the leaves are fibrous and hard to clean. Make infusions with water and oils. Lemon scent does not come through well in lye soap. It works better as a liquid in hand milling, but most of the lemon scent does not transfer.

- **Mint (*Mentha piperita*, *Mentha spicata*, etc.).** Tingly, fragrant, and invigorating; available as fresh or dried leaves, whole, cut for tea, or powdered. Add ground or flaked leaves to finished soap for texture. Make oil and water infusions for release of color. Green infusions will turn orange in the presence of lye, and the color will fade. Add ground mint to mint essential oil or other essential oils for a release of green color that will hold up slightly in lye soap. Use strong tea as liquid in hand milling for a slightly minty, light green effect.

- **Nasturtium (*Tropaeolum majus*).** Used as an astringent; it is best used fresh from the garden. Use the stems, flowers, leaves, and seeds. Make strong water and oil infusions. Use a water infusion as the liquid in hand milling for the best skin care benefit.

- **Rose (*Rosa damascena*).** Soothing and pleasing; available as dried and fresh petals. Use dried and ground in flakes or powder for texture. Use whole to infuse oils or water. Red rose petals make pink infusion, but the color doesn't last in the soap. Whole petals turn brown and ugly in soap.

- **Rosemary (*Rosmarinus officinalis*).** Refreshing and invigorating to the skin; available fresh or dried, powdered or chopped. Add powder or finely chopped dried leaves to soap for texture. Infuse in oils or water. If you are pregnant or nursing, consult your healthcare practitioner before using rosemary.

- **Saffron (*Crocus sativus*).** Saffron is the dried stamens of a certain kind of crocus. The herb is potently colored, fragrant, and extremely expensive. For very special soaps, use sparingly for color and texture. Releases its color into warm water.

- **Scented geranium (*Pelargonium graveolens*).** Available in a wide variety of fragrances, from rose and lime to chocolate mint! Fresh leaves are best, and the plant is easy to grow. Dried leaves add texture to finished soap. Dry well and grind thoroughly as the leaves are fibrous. Infuse oils and water with fresh scented geranium leaves. The scent will hold best if used as liquid in hand milling. Its astringent skin care benefit may survive other lye soapmaking techniques, but the scent won't.

- **Sweet woodruff (*Galium odoratum*).** Dried leaves exude the fragrance of fresh-mown hay with vanilla notes. It is available as dried leaves, whole, and powdered. To use in soap, infuse dried leaves in water or oil. Work dried leaves into hand-milled soap. The herb retains a subtle fragrance.

- **Yarrow (*Achillea millefolium*).** Helps to reduce pain and swelling of burns and abrasions; available as fresh or dried flowers, leaves, and stems. The dried and fresh flowers release a bright yellow dye into boiling water that fades almost completely—the leaves and stems to a lesser extent. It releases a bit of yellow when used as a lye infusion or steeped in oil.

BUYING FRESH HERBS

There are many different places to buy herbs. You can get common cooking herbs fresh or dried in the grocery. Other herbs are readily available as herbal tea, in bags, or bulk. Still other herbs, however, will take some sleuthing to find. A natural food store is a good place to start, and of course the Internet can be put to good use.

OTHER ADDITIVES

In addition to herbs, there are many things that you can add to your soaps to make them unique. Standing in the kitchen while making breakfast, you'll see all kinds of things you might want to try in soap. Oatmeal, honey, coffee, cocoa powder . . . the list goes on and on. Use your imagination and try out a few of these other additives: honey, glycerin, silk, grains, seeds, other exfoliants, and cosmetic clays. You may be pleasantly surprised by what you find.

Honey

Honey can be added to soap in small amounts. It is thought to be healing and moisturizing. Be very careful when you are making lye soap with honey as it will significantly increase the temperature of the curing soap.

In cold-process applications, forgo heavy insulation if you've used honey in your formula. Soapmakers have reported over and over again the "honey volcano" effect, where the soap overheats and gets a big, oozing crack down the center. Soap made with honey has even "climbed" right out of the mold.

Glycerin

Glycerin is a thick, sweet, clear liquid. It is a humectant moisturizer, meaning that it attracts water from the air. It is derived from plant or animal sources. The primary source of glycerin is commercial soapmaking. Saponification produces molecules of soap and molecules of glycerin, and the glycerin is removed to make the soap harder.

THE MEANING OF "GLYCERIN"

The word "glycerin" is often used as an adjective to describe transparent soap. Although it is a misnomer, as all soap is glycerin soap, it has come fully into the language. You can often find soap suitable for soap-casting projects labeled as glycerin soap.

In commercial soap, the glycerin is removed to make it longer lasting. You can add extra glycerin to your lye soap formula to create a more humectant bar. Or you can include palm kernel oil in your formula to boost the glycerin content in lye soap.

Silk

Silk is an easy-to-add protein that contributes, of course, a silky feel to your soaps. Silk is produced by silkworms that are fed on mulberry leaves. It has long been prized as a fiber for creating tough and elegant textiles.

You can purchase silk fibers, silk powder, and liquefied silk to add to your soap. You can even cut up silk fabric and dissolve it in the lye solution. Add silk powder and liquid silk to casting soap, liquid soap, and hand-milling projects.

Grains

You can add various forms of grain to your soap for texture. Cornmeal makes a rough scrub. Tapioca on the surface of a bar of casting soap makes a smooth, bumpy massager. And the most famous grain used in soap, oatmeal, is as popular as ever. Finely grind the oatmeal to release the skin-soothing properties for which oatmeal is so famous. If you want the look of the whole rolled-oat grain, use it sparingly since it can have sharp edges. Many soapers use baby oatmeal because it has a softer feel.

Seeds

Seeds of all kinds have been gaining popularity as soap additives. The two most readily available are coffee beans and poppy seeds. Others include cocoa powder (which comes from seeds) and berry seeds. Don't stop, though, at what you already have in your kitchen. Explore the growing possibilities.

Adding extremely finely ground coffee to the water with the lye makes a dark brown infusion and leaves tiny specks of brown in the finished bars. More coarsely ground coffee makes a good exfoliator. To release color in an infusion to use as the liquid in a lye soap recipe, the easiest thing to do is use cold, strong-brewed coffee. You can also use instant coffee.

Poppy seeds are great for a visual accent and because they are relatively round they're not too hard on skin. Cocoa powder comes from seeds as well. You can use it to enhance a recipe that contains cocoa butter and chocolate fragrance oil. You can also just use it as a finely textured colorant.

Berry seeds are a fairly new entrant into the exfoliant lineup. You can buy raspberry and strawberry seeds at soap supply companies.

Other Exfoliants

Other exfoliants include sand, pumice, vanilla bean powder, and bamboo powder. If you really want to exfoliate, sand and pumice are the way to go. Always remember that rough exfoliants like these are to be used on feet and very dirty hands only. Be sure to clean any sand you collect yourself. Only buy pumice that is intended for cosmetic use.

Bamboo powder is growing in popularity as a gentle and thorough exfoliator. You can use it in much the same way you do clays in your soap recipes. As with any exfoliator, less is usually more.

Cosmetic Clays

Kaolin, bentonite, rhassoul, and other kinds of cosmetic clays are put to good use in soapmaking. Clays are known in cosmetic applications as a drying agent for oily skin. In soap, you can also use them as a coloring agent.

Adding a cosmetic clay to a soap formula can help create a good bar for oily skin. You can add clay at a light trace in cold- and hot-process soap recipes. Blend the clay into a little bit of soap batter, then return the mixture to the rest of the mass, and blend in well. In hand milling, add the clay to the melting soap mass. For casting soap, add it when the soap is quite cool, as it will sink.

While the following table is not a comprehensive look at cosmetic clays, it will give you an idea of what is available.

KINDS OF COSMETIC CLAY		
Name	Appearance	Origin
Bentonite	Fine, grayish-white powder	USA
Green clay	Fine, green powder	France
Kaolin	Medium-fine, whitish gray powder	Cornwall
Rhassoul	Powder and lump you have to grind yourself	Morocco
Rose clay	Medium-fine, light red powder	France

CHAPTER SEVEN

FRAGRANCES YOU CAN PUT IN YOUR SOAP

When you pick up a bar of soap, the first thing you probably do is hold it to your nose and sniff. The packaging, color, and other visuals may attract you, but it's likely the scent that captures you. Some people choose unscented products. More, however, choose soap because they like the scent. You can scent your artisanal soaps in many ways. Two of the easiest are to add essential oils or fragrance oils. This chapter will tell you what you need to know about fragrance oils.

WHAT ARE FRAGRANCE OILS?

When shopping for fragrance oils to use in your soap creations, you'll be astounded by the vast array of scents available. From copies of famous perfumes to bubble gum, from ocean to tomato leaf, from incense to watermelon—the choice is spectacular.

Perfumery

When creating a scent, the perfumer draws upon talent, experience, intuition, and a vast knowledge of scent materials. Sometimes known as "a nose," a perfumer has an exceptional ability to combine chemistry with knowledge of the subtleties of scent to create a fabulous fragrance. Scent is the sense most closely linked to memory, and some of our most poignant memories are linked to the work of a perfumer.

The perfumer's palette consists of "notes." The primary notes are the top, middle, and base. The top note is the first impression. The middle is the scent you experience after the top note has dissipated, and the base note ties everything together, fixing it and leaving the most lingering scent. Of course these notes all work in concert to make the heart of the scent, but it is helpful to understand the note structure when talking about fragrance.

Description of Notes

Top notes are bright, light, and catchy. Florals, sweet fruit, and ozone are common top notes. They also tend to be fleeting, evaporating first, making way for the more complex middle and base notes. The top note doesn't leave completely but can be thought of as stepping back from center stage to take its place within the entire blend.

GET EDUCATED IN SMELLS

When you shop for fragrance oils, you may find it frustrating to have nothing but words to go on. Once you learn perfumery vocabulary, you can translate the written descriptions in a catalogue or on a website. You can educate yourself by going to a perfume counter. The salespeople can help you identify and name what you are smelling.

Middle notes mellow and enhance the brightness of the top note. They round it, fill it out, and support it. The middle note can support a top note by blending with it or by contrasting with it. If you layer a deeper floral under a lighter one, you have a middle note that blends. To support the top note through contrast, a sweet floral top note can be contrasted with a tangy middle note.

Base notes are frequently in the category of "fixatives." A fixative is a scent material that has an ability to linger and "stick" to the skin. Resins, moss, sticky grasses, and animal scents are fixative base notes.

CHOOSING FRAGRANCE OILS

There are many sources of fragrance oils. For the purpose of soapmaking, a fragrance must be "soap safe." A soap-safe fragrance oil is formulated to react well with the various soapmaking processes. A fragrance that isn't soap safe for lye soapmaking can cause a soap batch to seize—become clumpy and hard as soon as it is added. It can also make soap separate, curdle, discolor, or streak. The scents may fade or mutate, making them unsuitable for soapmaking.

There are some soapmaking fragrances that are safe for hot-process, soap-casting, or hand-milling applications only. Other fragrances cause visual problems with the finished soap. The most common cosmetic problem is discoloration. Responsible soapmaking suppliers will make this type of information clear in their catalogue materials.

Don't try fragrances from "fragrance bars" in bath and body shops in lye soapmaking. You can try them in soap casting and hand milling, but try them in small batches first. It is really best to stick with fragrances that are intended for soapmaking.

STORING FRAGRANCE OILS

Because fragrance oils contain no (or very little) natural plant matter, they may be safely stored at room temperature. Keep your oils in well-sealed glass bottles, carefully labeled. Put little labels on the tops of caps so you can easily find the one you want.

If a label looks like it's going to come off, it will, and it is better to replace it sooner than later. It is no good hunting through unlabeled fragrance bottles looking for what you need. Fragrance oils can smear even high-quality printing, so be sure to replace labels before they become unreadable.

TRY YOUR OWN FRAGRANCES

Even though there is a dizzying selection of fragrance oils available to you, you may still want to experiment with blending your own scents. Get a good book on fragrance and perfume making and see what you can learn. Also, just follow your instincts, your intuition, and your nose.

You can organize your scent cabinet to make it easy to find what you're looking for. If you have a few fragrances that you use all the time, keep them where they are easy to reach. You can organize your fragrances alphabetically, by scent family, by manufacturer, or any method you find useful. If you have fragrances that are useful for only one kind of soapmaking—soap casting, for example—be sure those are in a special location. You don't want to grab the melt-and-pour-only version of a fragrance when you need the one that is safe for cold process.

Scents are enticing, so keep your fragrances away from children, pets, and others who may be attracted to them. Never create the possibility of confusing vanilla fragrance with vanilla extract in the kitchen. Fragrance oils will damage or remove the finish from just about everything, so be sure to cover and protect your surfaces appropriately. Work with fragrances in a ventilated place, especially if you are sensitive to them.

UNDERSTANDING FRAGRANCE OIL FAMILIES

Over the ages, fragrances have been classified into groups. There are so many possibilities that the categories are constantly reinvented. Take some time to educate your nose, and you'll be able to classify fragrances in no time.

Floral

Some flowers have such well-known scents that the mere mention of the name conjures an immediate picture. Perhaps you have special memories connected to the scent of a certain flower. Although many of these scents are available as essential oils, they are usually quite costly. Some popular florals include carnation, frangipani, freesia, gardenia, honeysuckle, hyacinth, jasmine, lavender, lilac, magnolia, muguet (lily of the valley), pikake, plumeria, rose, tuberose, and violet.

Fantasy Floral

Scents inspired by the idea of a flower rather than the actual scent are referred to as "fantasy florals." Although these flowers may possess unique, sometimes fleeting, scents, they are frequently prized more for their visual rather than fragrant beauty. Fantasy floral fragrances include apple blossom, daffodil, daisy, heather, hibiscus, marigold, nasturtium, orchid, pear blossom, snapdragon, sunflower, and tulip.

Fruit

In recent years, fruit scents have come to the forefront of perfumery. Except for the citrus family, very few fruits are available in essential oils, so it has been the task of perfumers to create impressions of the wonderful fragrances of fruits in fragrance oils. Some perfumers have taken great flights of fancy, combining fruits with flowers, spices, and other treats.

Some examples include apple, apricot, apricot freesia, apricot quince, blackberry, black cherry, blood orange, blueberry, blueberry honeysuckle, cantaloupe, coconut, cranberry spice, cucumber melon, grapefruit, ginger fig, ginger lime, ginger papaya, guava, honeydew, huckleberry, kiwi, lemon, lemon fig, lime, mango, orange, peach, pear, pineapple, plum spice, pomegranate, pumpkin, raspberry cream, strawberry,

strawberry kiwi, tangerine, watermelon, and yuzu (Japanese grapefruit).

Sweets and Beverages

Another category of fragrance oils is sweets and beverages. There are many different kinds of some of these fragrances. You need to try a few vanillas, for example, to find your favorites.

VANILLA SOAP TURNS COLOR

Vanilla fragrance oil will turn most soap applications a shade of brown; in cold-process soap, the color can get very dark brown. It is the natural vanillin that causes the brown color. If the brown color bothers you, use the "non-discoloring" vanilla fragrance oils on the market.

You might try almond, brown sugar, cappuccino, chocolate, coconut, coffee, Dutch chocolate, gingerbread, green tea, hazelnut, red clover tea, or vanilla.

Other Fragrances

Some fragrances all but defy categorization. They often reflect the current fashion, with some becoming favorites. Such a favorite is "rain" and the related scents that became popular in the early 1990s. In the late 1990s, scents based on formerly overlooked botanicals, like tomato leaf, also began to turn up. Still others that have gained popularity again, such as amber, have long been at the heart of perfumery. Amber, fresh grass, oakmoss, ocean rain, rain, sweetgrass, sage, tomato leaf, and sandalwood are some current favorites.

FRAGRANCE TRENDS

Shifts in fragrance fashions do not come at regular intervals. A family of fragrance may be "in" for a long time before anything significant happens. There will always be the same general categories of flowers, herbs, fruits, and food, but sometimes one will take the forefront. Food aromas—particularly sweet ones like chocolate and vanilla—have bombarded the fragrance world in recent years.

Fragrance companies create slightly altered versions of classics in an attempt to boost sales without having to come up with something completely new. These "flankers" bring out one or more notes that played in the background of the original scent. This presents another learning opportunity for you; smell the original then smell the flanker and compare the two. What is different? Make notes, then read the literature on the companies' websites, at the counter, or ask the fragrance salesperson.

Of all the wonderful things about making your own soap, choosing your own fragrance—or choosing to go without—is one of the best parts. Don't be afraid to be original.

CHAPTER EIGHT

ESSENTIAL OILS YOU CAN PUT IN YOUR SOAP

In the study of soapmaking, one of the most interesting topics is essential oils. Unlike fragrance oils, which are synthetic, essential oils are the natural oils from plants. Like fragrance oils, essential oils contribute fragrance to your soap formulas, but they also have the benefit of aromatherapy, offering health benefits. The more you know about the properties of essential oils, the more you'll be able to create soaps that soothe, relax, invigorate, and improve mood.

WHAT ARE ESSENTIAL OILS?

When you hear the words "essential oils," you may think of aromatherapy. The term "aromatherapy" is becoming such a marketing buzzword that the actual meaning of the term has been obscured. Aromatherapy is more than just smelling something that makes you happy. Essential oils (the volatile oils of plants) have physiological effects on humans and other animals. In many countries, aromatherapy is used with other healing techniques to treat a variety of illnesses.

Whether or not soap is an effective method of delivery of aromatherapy is still debated in the soapmaking and aromatherapy communities. Some experts on essential oils insist that the therapeutic benefits of essential oils are lost during the soapmaking process. Heat is considered the enemy of the therapeutic efficacy of essential oils, and all soapmaking methods involve heat. Other experts on essential oils think there is still aromatherapeutic value in the essences when they are used in a soap recipe.

Soap may or may not be an effective delivery for aromatherapy, but essential oils can definitely contribute natural fragrance to handmade soap. Lavender soap, for example, has been a favorite around the world for generations. The sweet, herbal, and lightly floral scent of lavender essential oil helps create a soothing bathing experience.

ESSENTIAL OILS VERSUS FRAGRANCE OILS

Essential oils are the collected volatile oils of plants, while fragrance oils are synthetic (or created) fragrances. Essential oils are used for fragrance as well as their therapeutic properties. Fragrance oils often mimic the scents of plants, but although a synthetic fragrance oil might smell nice, it has no therapeutic benefit.

A BIT OF CHEMISTRY

Unlike the other oils and fats used in soapmaking, essential oils are not fatty acids. They evaporate readily, leaving no mark on a piece of paper. If you buy an "essential oil" and wonder if it is pure or not, drip a drop onto a piece of white paper. If it leaves a greasy mark after it has evaporated, it is probably impure.

If you decide to study the chemistry of essential oils, you'll find that there are often similar scents and therapeutic properties to oils that have a similar chemical makeup. For example, lemon balm, lemongrass, and lemon eucalyptus, although unrelated plants, all contain certain aldehydes that smell lemony. Roman chamomile, lavender, clary sage, and bergamot, some of the most commonly used essential oils, are all related through esters. Although they do not smell the same, these oils have similar effects on the body, and they blend well with each other.

METHODS OF ESSENTIAL OIL EXTRACTION

Essential oils are extracted from plant materials by methods that vary depending on the nature of the plant matter. Delicate blossoms are treated differently from woody stems and bark. Some of the most beautifully fragrant materials are too delicate to be captured, and others require processes so extensive that the cost becomes prohibitive.

There have been advances in essence-capture technology in the past decade that may yet bring us the heretofore elusive, unadulterated essences of those flowers and plants. Some of the most delicate essences are extracted using solvents, and since some of the solvent remains with the essence, these are thought to be useless in aromatherapy.

One of the earliest and most basic ways of extracting essential oils is the *enfleurage* method. The fragrant blossoms are spread on a base of animal or vegetable fat. When the fat has absorbed the essential oils, it is heated, and the fragrant materials are separated by evaporation, by solvent extraction, or both.

Distillation is an effective method of extraction, using a closed system of heat and evaporation. This method creates essential oils and waters infused with them in low concentrations called hydrolates or hydrosols.

There are other methods, including extraction by solvents. Aromatherapists prefer oils that have been as purely derived as possible, and although solvent extraction is useful and can produce good essential oils, there will be some undesirable solvent residue. Refer to the information provided by the distributor for extraction information.

STORING ESSENTIAL OILS

Essential oils are perishable and should be stored in dark glass containers in a cool place. As the bottle gets emptier, transfer the oil to a smaller bottle so the oil won't oxidize, causing decay. According to Marcel Lavabre's *Aromatherapy Workbook*, oils properly prepared and stored "can be considered fresh for three years after their extraction."

Essential oils can be very expensive, so it is important that you store them properly. If you find you're making a lot of soap and using essential oils, it really pays to order from online suppliers. An essential oil that costs $8 per quarter ounce in the health food store may cost only $40 a pound through an Internet soap supplier.

USING AROMATHERAPY

Whether or not essential oils retain their therapeutic properties after being exposed to the heat of soapmaking is questionable. You can still smell them, but the discrete biological elements that aromatherapists credit for some of the healing properties are probably destroyed along the way.

Regardless of the therapeutic value of soaps made with essential oils, there is no disputing the beauty of the aromas. There are many blends given in the recipes in this book, and they should just be a starting place. You will want to experiment and create the perfect blend of essential oils that is yours alone.

TABLE OF ESSENTIAL OILS				
Common Name	Latin Name	Cost Per Ounce	Origin	Extraction Method
Balsam of Peru	*Myroxylon balsamum var. pereirae*	$7.00–15.00	El Salvador	Steam distillation, solvent extraction
Benzoin	*Styrax benzoin*	$5.00–13.00	Tropical Asia	Resin is collected from trees, and then processed into powder or distilled into liquid resin

USING COMMON ESSENTIAL OILS

The following list includes readily available essential oils commonly used by soapers. It is by no means an exhaustive list, and you should not hesitate to experiment with others.

Appearance and Scent	Benefits	Uses in Soap
Thick, dark brown; vanilla-like, sometimes smoky	Itch relief, promotes cell growth, anti-inflammatory and antiseptic	Used as a base note and to fix other scents, particularly citrus; to incorporate it into a soap mixture, it needs to be dissolved in other essential oils or in a little bit of vegetable oil so it will disperse throughout the soap mixture
Thick, sticky fluid, golden-brown; warm, vanilla-like, resinous	Anti-inflammatory, antiseptic, astringent	Helps chapped skin, warming, soothing, calming, uplifting (noted to have caused dermatitis in sensitive individuals); benzoin essential oil and powdered benzoin are added to soap to bind the scent of citrus essential oils

Common Name	Latin Name	Cost Per Ounce	Origin	Extraction Method
Bergamot	*Citrus bergamia*	$7.00–25.00	Tropical Asia	Expressed oil from peel of fruit
Black pepper	*Piper nigrum*	$2.00–4.00	India, China	Distillation of the seeds
Cardamom	*Elettaria cardamomum*	$25.00–40.00	India, Central America	Steam distilled from seeds
Cedarwood: Atlas cedar; Virginia cedar; Texas cedar	*Cedrus atlantica, Juniperus virginiana, Juniperus mexicana*	$3.00–12.00	Morocco, Virginia, Texas	Virginia is distilled from sawdust; Atlas and Texas are from the needles and small branches
Chamomile: Roman chamomile; "German" chamomile	*Chamaemelum nobile, Matricaria recutita*	Roman $9.00–15.00, German $25.00–200.00	France, Morocco, Spain	Distillation of entire plant
Clary sage	*Salvia sclarea*	$5.00–9.00	Russia, United States	Steam distillation of stems and leaves
Clove bud	*Eugenia caryophyllata*	$5.00–10.00	Madagascar, Zanzibar, Indonesia	Distilled from dried buds
Coriander (cilantro)	*Coriandrum sativum*	$5.00–10.00	Europe	Distillation of seeds
Elemi	*Canarium luzonicum*	$9.00–25.00	Philippines, Central America, Brazil	Distillation of ripe seeds

Appearance and Scent	Benefits	Uses in Soap
Pale green; sweet, floral-citrus scent with almost woody undertones	Antiseptic, anti-spasmodic, anti-anxiety, digestive	Uplifting; use in citrus blends to round off top notes and help other citrus scents to "stick"; does not appreciably accelerate trace; potent photosensitizer
Yellow green; sweet, peppery, woody	Analgesic	Stimulating, warming, grounding, encouraging
Colorless to pale yellow; sweet, almost woody, spicy	Relieves nervous exhaustion	Stimulant, cleanser, mature skin
Atlas: gold color, smells deep, woody, and sharp; Virginia and Texas: mellow (because Virginia is a by-product of pencil-making, it is the least expensive and comes from the destruction of the entire tree)	Soothes irritated skin, antiseptic, helps control oiliness	Gives courage, clarity of thought; contributes a beautiful woody scent that combines well with citrus and with other woods and resins; middle-to-bottom note
German chamomile is blue, due to the azuline content; fragrance is lightly apple-like, fresh, and grassy; Roman is more herbal, more grass-like and is pale yellow	Antiseptic, anti-inflammatory, dermatitis, soothes itching, sedative	Soothing and calming
Clear to light yellow; slightly sweet and musky, lightly floral	regulates sebum, good for rashy, sensitized skin; estrogen balancer, antidepressant	Soothing and healing, helps in decision-making
Dark brown, very spicy and sweet	Antiseptic, analgesic, antiseptic	Warming, uplifting
Clear to light yellow	Natural deodorant, appetite stimulant, hormone balancer, restores equilibrium	Inspires creativity; bottom note
Sweet, balsamic fragrance, incense-like	Purifying, preserving	Soothing, spiritually uplifting, calms the nerves

Common Name	Latin Name	Cost Per Ounce	Origin	Extraction Method
Eucalyptus; lemon eucalyptus	*Eucalyptus globulus, Eucalyptus citriodora*	$5.00–10.00	Australia	Distillation of leaves
Fir	*Abies balsamea*	$5.00–10.00	Northeast US and Canada, Siberia	Distillation of branches
Frankincense	*Boswellia carteri*	$10.00–22.00	Southeast Arabia, northeast Africa	Extraction and distillation of pitch
Geranium	*Pelargonium graveolens, Pelargonium roseum*	$8.00–22.00	Egypt	Steam distillation
Ginger	*Zingiber officinale*	$6.00–23.00	China, India, Malaysia	Distillation of the root
Grapefruit	*Citrus paradisi*	$4.00–7.00	California	Expressed peel
Jasmine	*Jasminum officinale*	$78.00–172.00	France, Egypt, India	Enfleurage
Juniper	*Juniperus communis*	$12.00–20.00	Yugoslavia, Italy, France	Distillation of the berries and small branches
Lavender	*Lavandula angustifolia*	$5.00–11.00	Grown extensively in France and southern Europe	Steam distillation of the flowers

Appearance and Scent	Benefits	Uses in Soap
Clear to orange; very recognizable due to extensive use in cold remedies; stimulating	Clearing, antiseptic	Grounding, uplifting, stimulating; reduces excess oiliness
Fresh and coniferous	Antiseptic	Invigorating
Thick, amber liquid, sharp and resinous; good binder for other fragrances	Helps with prayer and meditation	Healing, firming
Clear liquid; strong, sweet, herby and rose-like; can be overpowering on its own	Astringent, anti-inflammatory	Good for alleviating tension and depression; holds up extremely well in soap
Golden yellow; spicy, sweet	Anti-nausea, anti-inflammatory	Stimulating and toning, enlivening, centering; use in small amounts in soap as it can be a dermal irritant in large amount
Yellow to pink, depending on variety	Diuretic, disinfectant	Toning, stimulating, uplifting; use in blends with other citrus and to brighten up other blends
Clear liquid; deeply, sweetly floral	Antidepressant, antianxiety	Heals irritated skin
Clear to pale green; crisp, resiny, sweet	Antiseptic, aids irritated skin	Relaxing
Clear to light green; herbal, sweetly floral	Analgesic, antispasmodic, acne dermatitis, insect repellent, antidepressant	Soothing, calming

Common Name	Latin Name	Cost Per Ounce	Origin	Extraction Method
Lemon	*Citrus limonum*	$5.00–15.00	California, Florida	Expressed peel
Lemongrass	*Cymbopogon citratus*	$4.00–10.00	India, Central America, Brazil	Distillation of the tall grass
Lime	*Citrus aurantifolia*	$5.00–7.00	Mexico, Florida	Expressed peel
Litsea cubeba	*Litsea cubeba*	$4.00–5.00	China	Distillation of the grass
Marjoram	*Origanum majorana*	$7.00–15.00	Spain, Hungary	Distillation of the plant while it is flowering
Myrrh	*Commiphora myrrha*	$20.00–25.00	Libya, Iran, southeast Arabia, northeast Africa	Distillation of collected resin
Myrtle	*Myrtus communis*	$8.00–11.00	Spain, Morocco	Steam distillation
Neroli (orange blossom)	*Citrus vulgaris*	$78.00–200.00	Egypt	Enfleurage of orange blossom
Nutmeg	*Myristica fragrans*	$6.00–10.00	Indonesia	Distillation of the nuts
Oakmoss	*Evernia prunastri*	$13.00–17.00	Yugoslavia	Distillation of lichen

Appearance and Scent	Benefits	Uses in Soap
Yellow liquid	Astringent, antiseptic, good for oily skin	Uplifting, enlivening; needs a boost in cold process from other citrus and citrus-like scents, and a resin like benzoin
Tan, with a sweet, herby lemony scent	Antiseptic, insect repellent, deodorant, disinfectant	Helps relieve stress; used not only for its own scent and actions but as a booster for citrus
Green; intensely tangy	Astringent, antiseptic, antianxiety	Uplifting; fills out a citrus blend and smells wonderful on its own
Yellow; heavily lemon, sweet rather than tangy	Antiseptic, deodorant	Uplifting; acts as a substitute and booster for citrus essential oils, which tend to be fleeting
Clear to light yellow; sweet, herbal, fresh	Antianxiety	Helps to relieve stress, pain, and tightness
Clear or yellow; spicy, woody	Anti-inflammatory, antiseptic, astringent	Centering and grounding
Fresh, sweet, camphoraceous	Antiseptic, stimulant, expectorant	Balancing, releases envy
Yellow; sweet, floral, citrusy, exquisite	Anti-depressant, sedative, emotional relief	Soothing, good for sensitive skin; you can use it in nearly-cool hot process and hand-milled soap so that you lose as little as possible of the scent and benefit
Clear to tan; sweet-spicy, peppery	Stimulant, anesthetic, antibacterial	Gentle stimulant, uplifting, encouraging; use in small amounts to round out a scent blend as it can be a dermal irritant
Dark brown, sticky, extremely viscous	Antiseptic	Grounding

Common Name	Latin Name	Cost Per Ounce	Origin	Extraction Method
Orange	*Citrus aurantium*	$3.00–10.00	California, Spain	Expressed peel
Palmarosa	*Cymbopogon martinii*	5.00–8.00	India, Africa, Madagascar	Distillation of grass
Patchouli	*Pogostemon cablin*	$5.00–11.00	India, Malaysia, Myanmar (Burma), Paraguay	Distillation of leaves after drying and fermentation
Peppermint; spearmint	*Mentha piperita; Mentha spicata*	$5.00–7.00	United States, England, France	Distillation of entire above-ground plant
Petitgrain	*Citrus aurantium*	$6.00–9.00	Spain	Distillation of leaves
Pine	*Pinus sylvestris*	$6.00–8.00	Russia, Balkans, Germany	Distillation of small branches
Rose	*Rosa centifolia, Rosa damascena*	$130.00–204.00	Bulgaria, Morocco, Turkey	Distillation of petals
Rosemary	*Rosmarinus officinalis*	$4.00–10.00	Mediterranean	Distillation of leaves and stems
Rosewood	*Aniba roseaodora*	$6.00–10.00	Brazil	Distillation of chopped wood

Appearance and Scent	Benefits	Uses in Soap
Strong orange scent	Antiseptic, antidepressant	Stimulating, cleansing, uplifting, warming; does not always last in cold-process soap; benefits from blending with other citrus, lemon-scented grasses and resins
Yellow; woody, rose-like, thinner scent than geranium	Antiseptic	Healing
Thick, dark brown; strong, unmistakable scent, sweet and musty	Fungicide, anti-anxiety	Stimulant, regenerating to the skin, relieves depression, encourages happiness; will color soap lightly tan
Clear to medium green; spearmint is more syrupy than peppermint, which has a sharper, clearer edge	Stimulating, antiseptic	In soap, it makes the whole soaping area smell like a toothpaste factory! Use in moderation as it can remain actively tingly even after going through the rigors of lye soapmaking
Clear to yellow; extremely tangy and slightly bitter	Clarifying, deodorant; helps with stress-related insomnia	Excellent foil for sweet florals; great blender
Clear liquid, fresh forest aroma	Astringent, toning	Centering and uplifting
Thick, amber liquid; rose scent, strong, floral, enduring	Helps sensitive, dehydrated, and aging skin	Perfect peace, love, and happiness
Nearly colorless; clear herbal with a bit of pine and sometimes eucalyptus	Healing of wounds and burns, dry scalp	Encouraging, memory enhancing
Clear to tan; woody, sweetly floral	Antidepressant, antibacterial, antiseptic	Releasing, grounding, calming, good for sensitive or mature skin

Common Name	Latin Name	Cost Per Ounce	Origin	Extraction Method
Sandalwood	*Santalum album*	$22.00–49.00	India, Nepal	Steam distillation of sawdust
Tangerine	*Citrus reticulata*	$5.00–9.00	Florida, California	Expressed peel
Tea tree	*Melaleuca alternifolia*	$4.00–13.00	Australia	Distillation of the leaves
Vetiver	*Andropogon muricatus*	$8.00–16.00	Caribbean, Haiti	Distillation of the roots
Ylang ylang	*Cananga odorata genuina*	$9.00–22.00	Madagascar	Steam distillation of flowers

Appearance and Scent	Benefits	Uses in Soap
Thick, pale amber to brown liquid; beautiful, woody-sweet fragrance	Antidepressant, anti-inflammatory, antispasmodic	Healing, soothing, moisturizing; helps center for meditation; one of the most popular synthetics due to cost and desire not to further endanger habitat
Yellow-orange liquid; sweet and tangy, honey-like citrus	Helps heal acne, good as an astringent tonic, helps relieve insomnia	Brings a sweetness to citrus blends
Light yellow to clear; very strong antiseptic scent	Extremely useful antiseptic; helps to clear headaches	Strengthening, uplifting
Thick, dark brown; earthy, ashy, burned wood smell	Anti-inflammatory, especially for acne	Grounding, centering
Yellow, viscous; strong, intense fragrance; floral, sweet, syrupy	Antidepressant, sedative, stimulant, relieves nervous tension	Good for oily skin; like geranium, it can hold its own in soapmaking; makes a beautiful foil for tangy lime and herbaceous lavender

FINE FRAGRANCE SOAP PROJECT

You can make some incredible aromas with a selection of these essential oils, and you can enhance, deepen, and beautify them further with the inclusion of just two or three pricy items. Once you graduate to using fine fragrances, you need perfumer's alcohol and pipettes to work with the precious oils in a way that doesn't waste them. After you've used a pipette to move the scent material to the blending container, get as much of it back into the original bottle as possible. When you've done that, use perfumer's alcohol in a small bottle to rinse the pipette. After you've cleaned the pipettes of each material, you'll have an amazing smelling eau de toilette in the bottle.

Here's a list of common essential oils:

- Clary sage

- Lavender

- Orange

- Patchouli

- Peppermint

- Rose geranium

- Rosewood

Here are some uncommon, yet reasonably priced, aroma sources:

- Balsam Peru

- Benzoin resin

Here are some precious aromas that are a good place to start:

- Jasmine absolute

- Labdanum absolute

- Neroli essential oil

- Rose absolute

- Tuberose concrete

Make a 1-pound batch of soap using the luxury fixed oils you've had stashed. When your soap is at a thin trace, divide it into small molds. Add your perfume to the small bars-to-be drop by drop, stirring well to incorporate the scent throughout. Do one with the top notes, one with the heart, and one with the base, a couple of bars with the full fragrance, and the rest with single notes of the blend.

When you are experimenting, make careful notes of what went into each bar. When you are assessing the aromas later, take note of which aroma survived the best, partially, or not at all. When you tinker with micro-batches, you get a variety of luxury soaps and an excellent set of lessons on how to put your precious aroma materials to their best use in soapmaking.

CHAPTER NINE

COLOR FOR YOUR SOAP

Any soap is beautiful, but when you add color, you get the added bonus of making soap decorative, pleasing, soothing, or exciting. Often, working color into your formula makes everything come together.

UNDERSTANDING COLOR THEORY

We don't need to go into too much detail about the theory of color. Instead, let's start with a valuable tool: the color wheel. You can purchase one at an art supply store, or you can make one with some heavy white paper and a medium-sized box of crayons. A simple color wheel can help you a great deal when working on color for your soap projects.

To make your own color wheel, draw a circle with a black crayon. Divide the circle into three even pie shapes. With the clock as a model, put yellow at 12:00, red at 4:00, and blue at 8:00. These are the primary colors that cannot be created by mixing other colors. Next come the secondary colors, which are mixtures of two primaries. Yellow and red make orange; red and blue make purple; blue and yellow make green. Select those colors from your crayon box and draw lines with each between the corresponding positions on the wheel.

Then we have the tertiaries. Remember wondering what was the difference between blue-green and green-blue? Well, that's what you're working with now, colors with two names. Think of the first word in a two-name color as an adjective; it describes the second word. So, find the orange-yellow crayon. It is yellow with orange in it. Then comes yellow-orange, which is orange with yellow in it. Work your way around your color wheel, making a line or wedge of color to go with each name. When you're done, it will look like a circular rainbow.

Complementary Colors

Now see which colors are opposite each other. Start with the primaries. Yellow is opposite secondary purple, red is opposite secondary green, and blue is opposite secondary orange. You can see a pattern: in pairs of opposites, called complementary colors, secondaries are the complements of primaries. In soapmaking, adding a little of a color's complement, called "complementary mixing," is an extremely useful way to make a vibrant color less so. It is often called "graying out."

The gray-out factor presents a challenge when you want to create soap in shades of purple. There will normally be a yellow to yellow-green cast to your base oils. This will usually lighten with time to a creamy yellow or just cream color. Think of the complementary pair of yellow and purple. When you add violet oxide, for instance, you will achieve a grayed-out yellow, then a grayed-out purple before achieving a clear purple. It will take a lot of purple pigment to compensate for the complementary mix.

DON'T OVERDO IT

When experimenting with the gray-out factor, you need to remember that the yellowness of the soap will decrease as the soap cures, so you need to be sure not to overdo your compensatory mixing.

WRITING COLOR STORIES

The next part of the color-theory lesson is all about stories—color stories. Think of an advertising campaign for makeup, clothing, craft supplies, or home décor. There will be an identifiable unifying idea behind the campaign. For example, the "New Fall Colors" may consist of colors that make you think of turning leaves, harvest, and cooler weather. Such colors may be "Harvest Gold," "Fading Yellow," "Rusty Brown," and "Deep Wine." This is called a color story.

The color stories you create for your soaps can be as straightforward as traditional color combinations—for example, pink and blue soaps made for a baby shower. You may want to tell a story in color about the herbs that you've used in your soap. Or you may want just the perfect shade to pull your towels, tile, and paint together in your bathroom.

Creating a Color Story

As an exercise, go into your bathroom and look at the color details. List the colors of the paint, fixtures, tile, wallpaper, and decorative accents. This list of colors forms the foundation of your color story. For example, let's create the color story of a hypothetical bathroom. The paint is very pale pink; the tile is white with a thin, pale green-blue accent border. The fixtures are white, and the towels are light sage green.

Using the color wheel, look at the nature of this color story. The light pink and the light sage green are unsaturated versions of the complementary colors red and green. Blue-green is next to green on the color wheel, on the way to blue. So, you've got a pastel complementary scheme with a tertiary accent.

AVOID MESSES

Try to keep the amount of colorant in your soaps to a level that will not make a mess on washcloths, in the shower, and in the tub. Very rarely will a soap colorant color your skin, but it can happen. Follow usage guidelines and common sense. Luckily, since the pigment is delivered to the surface by soap, it will usually wash out. But not always!

You'll be setting the soap on the white sink or tub. It will probably be seen with the pink paint and a light sage-green washcloth in the background. Since the color scheme is low contrast, you will probably want to keep the soap low contrast as well. A pale pink soap in the same color range as the paint, with a sage green swirl, would be soft and pretty and feminine. A light sage-green soap with a thin, light green-blue swirl would add a touch more color and tie the blue and green together. Try this exercise in your own bathroom. It will be very interesting to see what you come up with.

USING COLOR IN SOAP

The way you incorporate color into your soap depends on the kind of soap and the kind of colorant you're using. You can color the soap directly by adding the colorant to the soap mixture. You can also add pieces of colored soap as in the "chunking" and confetti techniques. Here, we'll talk about how to use color in each of the soapmaking techniques.

Coloring Cold-Process Soap

When you're working with cold-process soap, a number of colorants will fade, change, or disappear altogether due to their reaction to active lye. Natural plant dyes will be obliterated except for a few tenacious examples. Certain food colorants will change color entirely.

Fortunately, there are also many kinds of colors that will hold up through the rigors of the cold-process method. A few plant dyes, including some spices, produce colors ranging from subtle to bright. Ultramarines and oxides hold up very well, as do many micas.

Coloring Hot-Process Soap

In the hot-process techniques, you can add color after the soap is neutral, so you have more choices available than in cold process. You can often use less colorant, with more predictable results.

Getting colorants distributed evenly in hot-process soap is difficult. When you add color at the end of the cooking period, you are trying to add it to a very thick, sticky mixture. Some of the soap has cooled into tiny lumps, while some of it is fluid enough to accept the colorants.

Experiment with different ways of incorporating color into hot process. One thing to try is to remove a small portion of the mass you want to color, mix the colorant into that, and then mix the colored portion back into the rest. Give it, and yourself, a good workout trying to get the color evenly distributed.

In hot processing, and in fact all lye soapmaking techniques, you can add some color elements from the beginning of the process. You may use an infusion of an herb to mix with the lye, or you may use an oil that has been colored with herbs. These herbal infusions will usually take quite a beating in the process, but there are herbal colorants that transmit well this way.

COLORS IN HOT AND COLD

With hot process, if the soap is still slightly alkaline, colorants that fade in alkaline soap will do the same here. Chances are about fifty-fifty that a colorant said not to be stable in cold process will be stable in hot.

You can also add mineral pigments to the early stages of making lye soap. Ultramarines and oxides perform beautifully when added with the lye to the water to make a tinted lye solution. Keep in mind that the entire batch will be that color. You can make two separate batches simultaneously using color in this way, and swirl them together, avoiding the complication of adding colorant later. You can also vary the color at the end with more colorant, or pieces of differently colored soap. Planning ahead pays off.

Coloring Casting Soap

Soap casting is where color really takes center stage (see Chapter 11 about soap casting). The premade soap base will accept just about any pigment. Herbs will eventually turn brown in any soap, but in soap casting, they'll keep their color for a little while.

You can use different kinds of coloring together in the same projects. Combining liquid soap dye with a little mica makes a very simple and beautiful soap-casting project. Ultramarines and plant materials can be used together to great effect. Again, imagination is the key.

It doesn't take much pigment for transparent soap to go from clear to opaque, or so saturated with color that little light goes through. Often, less is more. Take advantage of the beauty of the way light passes through the soap, especially with mica.

ENJOYING NATURAL COLOR SOURCES

Nature provides us with beautiful colors that can be applied to coloring soap. You can add plant material directly to the soap mixture to create not only color but texture as well. Most plant material that starts out green will eventually turn brown. However, some botanicals—calendula petals, for example—retain their color when added at the end of the process. You can also use dried herbs in hand-milling products if you really want the color to stay for a while. Be sure that when you're adding herbal ingredients directly into the soap, you remove sticks, twigs, and other sharp parts of the plant.

VOLATILE OILS

Highly sensitive individuals should avoid plants with lots of volatile oils such as rosemary, the mints, and even lavender. Look to herbal reference books for sensitivity information and remember that it is always wise to err on the side of caution.

To get the color from the plant matter into your soap, you can use a variety of methods. Infusing oil and water with a high concentration of the color herb creates a usable dye. Be sure to record the amounts, temperatures, and length of infusion time so you can repeat what works. There are a few commercially available plant dyes.

There are quite a few plants that work as colorants for soap, but annatto seed and alkanet root are some of the most easily used. Since plants vary from season to season and crop to crop, you should test each new supply you purchase. The following exercise in making your own natural dyes will start you on your way to further experimentation. For this recipe, use two heatproof clear containers that will hold at least 2 cups.

✿ ━ ANNATTO SEED INFUSION ━ ✿

Annatto seeds produce a vibrant orange dye. It will fade to various shades of lighter gold and yellow in soap. Annatto is sold as "annatto seed," but it isn't really seeds. It is little beads made of the dried fruit. They are very hard and difficult to grind. To get color out of it, it needs to be exposed to warmed oil.

4 tablespoons annatto seed   **1 cup distilled water, boiling**   **1 cup olive oil**

---

1. Place 2 tablespoons of the annatto seed in each of the heatproof containers.

2. Pour the water over the annatto in one container.

3. Add the oil to the annatto in the other container. Microwave on high for 1 minute. Check for color—if the annatto has released a lot of orange, you don't need to continue heating. If necessary, microwave on high for 1 more minute. (Watch the oil carefully through the second minute. If it starts to bubble, take it out.)

4. Place the two containers of annatto infusion side by side and compare the colors. You'll observe a clear golden color to the water infusion. The oil infusion will be a very deep orange.

FOOD AND COSMETIC DYES

You can use liquid food coloring from the grocery to color your soap. Most food colors will fade with even a little exposure to sunlight, so just know that your soaps will fade. Since the colorings are liquid, you need to allow for the extra liquid you'll be adding to the recipe.

You can also buy food and cosmetic dyes in very concentrated powder form. They produce brilliant colors, and one tiny package of powder goes a long, long way. Take care when using them that you don't get them on anything you don't want dyed. In general, you add a tiny amount of dye powder to a teaspoon of warm water. You add the concentrated color in small amounts until you get the color you want. It is easy to go overboard, so watch carefully how much you add.

Gel Colorants

Liquid gel colors are an invaluable method of color delivery. They work extremely well in soap casting and can be applied to lye soap processes as well, with varying results. Again, learning through experimentation is how you can predict what will happen.

The gel colorants come in an incredible array of colors. Many of them are grouped into color stories and are available as kits. There are triple-strength colors that are more concentrated than the others. You can also get gel tones in primary colors so that you have unlimited color-blending powers at your fingertips.

Lab Colors

Since 1999, Bramble Berry soapmaking supply company (*www.brambleberry.com*) has been offering Lab Colors. They are super-concentrated food and cosmetic dyes with exacting directions about how to use them. They come in small portions, which are diluted in hot water and stored in bottles to use as needed. There are many colors, including a "basic twelve" that can be used to blend a wide variety of colors. The colorants come with a usage booklet and a color-blending chart, showing color blends for high- and low-pH products. So, the trouble with food and cosmetic colors being unpredictable is eliminated as the colors were particularly formulated for use with high-pH cold-process soap.

Working with Lab Colors can take some getting used to, but when you have facility with them, you'll wonder how you did without them. If there are color blends you frequently use, pre-mix them into smaller containers to make things simple. For people who want to spend less time experimenting with color and more time actually working with color, this is a great system.

Mineral Pigments

You can get incredible color by using mineral pigments such as ultramarines and oxides. These are the basic pigments used in cosmetics and by artists who blend their own paint. Be sure the mineral pigments you use are designated for soap and cosmetic application. Don't buy them at an art supply store, since you don't know if they are safe to use on the skin. Responsible soap supply houses will sell only the kinds of pigments that are safe to use in soap.

If you are going to make soap of all one color, you can add the mineral pigment with the lye to the water to make a colored lye solution. This way, the color will not be affected negatively by the lye and the color will be dispersed throughout the soap.

You may also add the mineral pigment at the end of the stir. Mix the amount of pigment you want to use and blend it with a teaspoon of hot water. Blend it well. Strain it if there are stubborn clumps that won't dissolve. Remove a portion of the soap to be colored and mix the pigment mixture into it. Add it back to the main mass and stir well to evenly incorporate. Do this for as many colors as you want to use in a batch.

MICA AND GLITTER

In addition to adding color to soap, you can also add special features such as mica and glitter. Mica is, quite simply, beautiful. It is sparkly, shimmery, and even pearly, and comes in a dazzling array of colors. It is put to best effect when used in a transparent or translucent application. You can use it to color opaque soaps, but the shimmer shows up best when it has light hitting it from more than one side.

Micas are loosely classified as sparkles, highlights, and pearls. Some are two-tone, showing one color when you look at the soap from one direction and another when you look at it another way. Making a group of soaps in three versions of the same color—sparkle, highlight, and pearl—can make a beautiful presentation. You can also do this in one soap for an elegant monochromatic effect.

Adding Mica

Add micas in much the same way as you would add mineral pigments. Stir the amount of color you want to use into a little of the soap, then incorporate that back into the main mass. Some micas lose their color completely in the high alkalinity of lye soap, especially cold process. Your mica supplier will have this information for you.

When using mica in casting soap, add it a little at a time, as you can easily add more. If you find you have more than you want, dilute the over-colored soap with more plain. Unless you've gone really overboard with the color, this will help you get back to the depth of color you want.

Adding Glitter

Glitter is very beautiful in transparent soaps. Use a small amount for a delicate twinkle. Use a lot for an outrageous sparkle. If you give soap with glitter to someone, make sure that they know not to use it as a facial soap, as it is easy to get soap in your eyes when you wash your face. It would be very easy to get a tiny piece of glitter in your eye that would then scratch your cornea as you blink.

Be sure the glitter you use in your soap is cosmetic grade. Your soapmaking supplier will be sure to only sell the right kind of glitter. Like any material, do your research. Make decisions and use what pleases and makes sense to you.

Glitter is generally made from polyester and will melt like plastic if exposed to high heat. You need to take this into consideration when adding it to hot soap mixtures. Add glitter to casting soap that is about 130°F. If you add it as an accent in cold process, add it at trace, as you would a spice or herb. In hot process, add it at the very end, when the soap is coolest.

Since pieces of glitter are bigger than mica or mineral pigment, sprinkling it right into the soap works well. Be sure not to throw it in all at once, or it will clump. If you get clumps, just break them up on the side of the pan with your spoon.

CHAPTER TEN

LIQUID AND CREAM SOAPS

By extending the hot process, you can make liquid, transparent, and cream soaps. They can be very difficult to make, but it's well worth the effort because you get homemade soap in beautiful liquid, transparent, and creamy forms. Making these soaps from scratch is sure to elicit compliments from your guests.

MAKING LIQUID SOAP

To make liquid soaps, you take the hot-process soapmaking techniques, make a few ingredient adjustments, and then go a few steps further. You make the caustic solution with water and potassium hydroxide, add it to warmed oils, and then you cook it until it is neutral. The mass of neutralized soap is the concentrate from which you will make the liquid soap.

You will measure out this neutral soap gel and melt it into water. You can keep the extra gel-like base in a sealed plastic container in the refrigerator (well labeled!) and make up more liquid soap as needed. This works well, because like any soap, liquid soap has a shelf life. It's better to mix up more as you need it than have an entire batch sitting around resolidifying or getting rancid.

Instead of sodium hydroxide, you will use potassium hydroxide to make liquid soap. The soap paste with which you are left at the end of the first cook will have a texture like gummy jelly. Melting the paste into water makes the liquid soap.

VARIETY IS THE SOAP OF LIFE

One benefit of making small batches of liquid soap from the stored base is the ability to create variety. For instance, you can make some in sage green for the kitchen, light blue for the powder room, and soft rose for the master bath.

LIQUID SOAP IN SLOW COOKER

For this recipe, use a 3½-quart slow cooker. If you use too small a slow cooker for the batch, you increase the chances of overheating, overflowing, and the "volcano" action of the cooking soap. You can make liquid soap in a double boiler or with the oven hot-process techniques, too.

➤ **YIELDS ABOUT 3 POUNDS OF PASTE, WHICH WILL DILUTE TO ABOUT 6 POUNDS OF LIQUID SOAP** ◄

22 ounces coconut oil
4 ounces castor oil
1 ounce jojoba oil

16 ounces water
6.25 ounces potassium hydroxide

Rubbing alcohol in small spray bottle to control bubbles

1. Set the slow cooker to high. Place the coconut oil, castor oil, and jojoba oil into the slow cooker. Cover to hold in heat. Melt the oils.

2. Place the water in a heatproof container and sprinkle the potassium hydroxide into the water. Stir until all the potassium hydroxide is dissolved. (This mixture won't get as hot as the lye solutions for solid soap since you're using more water.) Without waiting for it to cool, add the potassium-water solution to the oils by pouring it in a thin stream, stirring constantly and carefully to fully combine the mixture.

3. Using an immersion blender, blend the mixture to trace. Keep the head of the blender fully immersed to avoid blending air into the soap batter.

4. When the mass starts to thicken, the mixture will thicken fast—it may just become nearly solid! Remember that this will happen all of a sudden, so watch that you don't burn out the blender by not paying attention.

5. Let the paste cook until it's translucent. (This will take about 3 hours.) Stir the neutralizing soap every 30 minutes by folding the soap with a firm yet careful hand, incorporating the puffy areas into the center. (Keep the slow cooker covered as much as possible. The longer you leave the lid off, the more water will evaporate, which will throw the formula out of balance.)

(continued on next page)

6. After 3 hours, test to see if the soap is neutral. Scrape a small portion onto a folded-up paper towel. Drip a couple of drops of phenolphthalein onto the soap. If it turns bright pink, it needs more cooking. If it is clear with just a little pink, you're ready to move on.

7. If you're going to make finished liquid soap right away, measure out the amount you want to dilute and store the rest. Take the finished paste out of the slow cooker and let it cool in a glass or metal bowl. When it's cool, put the amount you wish to store into a heavy zip-lock bag.

8. Place the paste that you wish to make into liquid soap in a stainless steel pan over direct heat on your stove, to melt the paste into the water. Use equal parts paste and water. Although it will produce some foam, boiling is the best way to get it started.

Be sure the pan is an appropriate size for the batch you are making. One pound of paste and 2 pounds of water will fit perfectly in a standard 4-quart saucepan.

9. Bring the paste and water to a boil. Reduce the heat and simmer, uncovered, for 15–30 minutes. You need to stay with it, making absolutely sure it doesn't boil dry. It may be tempting to put a lid on, but it is better to leave the lid off, because the boil-over potential is very great, even if you keep the heat the same.

10. When the soap paste has dissolved, remove the pan from the stove and stir to incorporate as much foam as you can.

11. Spritz the surface with rubbing alcohol to clear any bubbles that remain. (Do not do this near a gas range!) Add color and fragrance, if you like.

If you've used sodium hydroxide, you'll notice that this stir to trace is different. It is very opaque and milky right away, yet very thin. You have to use the hand blender for action to get it to start tracing. When it does, it happens all of a sudden. Big bubbles will start to kick up when it's about to firm up.

You can divide the finished soap into small amounts and experiment with color and scent. Some fragrance oils and essential oils have color of their own, so add them before you add the colorant. Liquid food colors work perfectly well and look best when used in small amounts. The liquid soap will be somewhat yellow, so remember this when working out your color plan.

Homemade liquid hand and body soap is similar to the kind you buy at the store. You can pump or squeeze it in a similar way, and it foams nicely on the skin, especially if you use a sponge or a loofah. Where most liquid soaps made at home fall short is if you try to use them for shampoo, shower gel, or bubble bath.

Of course, you can use the recipe as shampoo to see how you like it. Many people prefer the feeling they get from a detergent shampoo to the feel of handmade liquid soap shampoo. You may find, though, that you love it! Handmade liquid shampoo can leave some people's hair feeling oily, stiff, dry, or just strange.

All shampoo will eventually leave a buildup on your hair, and homemade soap will do this faster. It is a good idea to use a vinegar rinse at least once a week to take care of this. You can make wonderful herbal vinegars that you'll use highly diluted in water. Infuse 2 cups of white or apple cider vinegar with ¼ cup dried lavender, rosemary, or other herb of your choice. Let it infuse for a week. Use 1 tablespoon of strained, infused vinegar for each 8 ounces of water. You can put this in a big squeeze bottle when you know you're going to need it and keep it in the shower. Use up the diluted solution within a few days.

You can try making bubble bath with the liquid soap, too. To get better bubbles, try adding 1–3 teaspoons of glycerin per pound of diluted soap. Depending on the water in your area, this may or not produce big bubbles.

USING FOAMING BASES

If you want to make your own shampoo, shower gel, and bubble bath, you can buy clear, unscented shampoo, shower gel, and bubble bath. These premade bases are technically not soap, but they are used for cleansing, they bubble, and they present opportunities for creativity. You warm them and make additions, but instead of pouring them into molds like you would with casting soap, you pour them into plastic bottles. A lineup of beautifully colored and scented shampoo, shower gel, and bubble bath can look like shiny jewels on the edge of the tub. Think about how you can create coordinating looks for your bathrooms, coded colors for each type of product, or even each family member.

If you want to choose one base to use universally, choose a shampoo base, as you can certainly use that as a body wash, and often as a bubble bath, although you have to try each one as they differ in how well they hold up in the bath.

Choosing a Container

Transparent, squeezable plastic bottles that are made of PET plastic are ideal. The kind of plastic is important, because there are many plastics that will not stand up to fragrance oils or essential oils. Look for the initials PET on the bottom of the bottles if you reuse bottles you already have, or buy them at the drug store. If you order from an online soapmaking supplier, look in the product descriptions to be sure you get PET. Get PET bottles even if you don't intend to use scent material, because chances are, you will eventually.

FOAMING BASES AND DETERGENTS

Foaming bases are primarily water, detergents, surfactants, and skin or hair conditioners. Detergents are commonly derived from coconut, palm, and olive oils, or the separated fatty acids of those oils. You'll often find fatty acids, such as sodium lauryl sulfate, at the top of the list of ingredients in shampoo, bubble bath, and dishwashing liquid.

Two- and 4-ounce bottles are excellent choices, especially when you are first starting, because you aren't committed to a large amount of any one experiment. For most foaming bases, flip-tops are perfect. You can also get pumps, and they are usually more useful for 8- and 16-ounce bottles (they can topple the smaller bottles). Most packaging suppliers sell bottles and caps separately, so be sure to order both. Two favorite bottle shapes are called Boston Round and Cosmo Oval. It is partly a matter of aesthetic preference, but the Cosmo Ovals are easier to squeeze.

Adding Colors and Scents

Like so much in soapmaking, your options with foaming bases are virtually unlimited. You can add color, fragrance, and other additives. You can choose sheer colors; shimmery, pearly micas; and even glitter. The crystal-clear appearance of unscented liquid bases can be accented beautifully with just about any kind of cosmetic colorant. Gel color, Lab Colors, mica, mineral pigment, and food coloring from the grocery store are all great choices. Start with a small amount of color and work your way up. Keeping it relatively sheer takes advantage of the way light passes through the liquid.

Aromas from fragrance oils are wildly varied, and you can decide how strong or how light you want the scent to be. Using essential oils and other natural aromas, you can create truly aromatherapeutic products for you to use daily and as need arises. Most bases will take any cosmetic fragrance material: fragrance oils, essential oils, or blends of both. Some suppliers suggest the use of a solubulizer to hold the scent material in suspension and keep it from making the base cloudy or runny. Whether you need it or not depends on the kind of base and the kind and quantity of fragrance material. Get a small bottle when you order your base and scents; that way you'll have it if you need it, and if you don't you won't have a large amount of something you don't need.

Other things you could add to your foaming base include scrubs like bamboo granules and powdered loofah, jojoba spheres, and clays that add color, scent, and texture. Additionally, you can add the foaming bases to basic handmade beauty formulas, such as sugar scrubs, to add foam and rinsability.

COLORING AND SCENTING UNSCENTED BASES

Try the products and make notes on what you like, what looks too bright,
smells too strong, what foams, and what doesn't.

Customized liquid bases   **Essential oils**   **Funnel**
Glass measuring cup   **Fragrance oils**   **Bottles and closures**
Spatulas   **Solubulizer**
Cosmetic-grade colorants   **Other additives as desired**

1. Measure out the amount of base you're going to need into the glass measuring cup. You can do a quick one-off batch to start, or maybe try a variety of color and scent combinations. Whichever you choose, employ the mise en place technique to minimize clutter and keep you focused on creating.

2. Warm the base in the microwave in 10-second intervals, stirring well with a spatula after each heating. You don't want the base to be hot and totally liquid. You're just warming it to make it easier to incorporate additives and pour into bottles.

3. When the base is warmed enough to be easy to pour, add your color, oils, solubulizer, and other additives. Stir well. Use the funnel to help you fill the bottles. If you want to make a variety of scents and colors and additives, you can pour plain warmed base into the bottles, then make the additions. Close the cap and shake well to incorporate the ingredients.

4. Set the bottles (with caps open) out to cool. Any cloudiness should have subsided within a few hours, if not right when cooled.

5. If you find the base is runny after settling, try adding more solubulizer at the supplier's recommended amount, which is usually the same amount as the fragrance material.

This kind of crafting is moving away from soapmaking and into handmade toiletries. If you've been wondering about lotions and other potions, this is a good jumping-off place. For a quick project, make a room spray with 8 ounces of water, and ¼ teaspoon each of scent material and solubulizer. Put in a spray bottle and shake well before using.

MAKING TRANSPARENT SOAP

A great number of people who want to make their own soap are drawn to transparent soap because of its beauty. With some alterations in ingredients, you can use the hot-process technique you've already learned to make incredible transparent soap. This from-scratch soap cannot be easily melted and molded, but it is beautiful in its own right.

The addition of sugar and alcohol are the best ways to make transparent, or at least translucent, soap at home. Commercially, the process involves pressure and extreme temperatures. At home, it is an extension of the cold- and hot-process techniques.

If you are tempted to make transparent lye soap your first project, resist the temptation, or at least have an experienced soaper help you. Lye soapmaking from scratch is daunting enough the first time without the added variables introduced with this technique.

The addition of the sugar and alcohol alters the way the molecules crystallize, creating a clear appearance. You may not always get clear soap—it may often be cloudy or translucent, but it will always be unique and beautiful. The soap is perfectly good to use even if it is cloudy.

Although you cannot easily melt and pour this kind of soap, you can cut it into pieces and use it as chunks and other fancy shape details in cold-process soaping. You can do this kind of fancy work with glycerin soap base, but you may have better luck with the chunks staying in place if you make your own lye-based translucent soap, due to the similarity of the makeup of the soap.

Transparent soap made through the hot-process method lets you control the ingredients, just as you do with opaque soap. It can be a tricky process, with a lot of trial and error, but the benefits are great, not the least of which is the pride you feel when you say, "Yes, I did make that!"

Transparent Soap Equipment

You will need the usual lye soap equipment, plus hot-process equipment, plus a few things especially for transparent soap. You can use the same molds you've been using. Of course, the safety precautions apply.

> **GET A FIRE EXTINGUISHER**
>
> *If you don't already have a fire extinguisher in your soapmaking area, you must get one before making transparent soap with alcohol. Make sure it is charged and within reach. You shouldn't have to find out where it is when you desperately need it.*

If you have a gas range, don't use it. Get a two-burner buffet range. It is not worth the potential danger and worry to use alcohol over an open flame.

Transparent Soap Ingredients

To make transparent soap, you'll make a simple syrup of water and sugar and add it at the same time as the alcohol. To help ensure the transparency of the finished product, the base oils need to maintain clarity. Highly saturated oils that look opaque, for example, will make the soap less transparent if used in high amounts. Excess fats, so desirable in other lye soap, will make this soap cloudy, so you cannot superfat the way you do with other methods.

For this reason, transparent soap recipes use a high level of lubricating castor oil and limit the coconut oil. Castor oil is a major component in transparent soapmaking. It is transparent, provides lather, and is lubricating to the skin. You need some coconut oil for cleansing and lather. Palm oil is for the production of stearin, which makes the bar hard.

It is harder to keep the temperatures at the right level with a batch under 4 pounds, so there is no 1-pound recipe given for transparent soap. The amounts of ingredients must be precise, and that is more difficult to do in such a small recipe. If you decide to increase the following recipe, you must use a proportionately larger slow cooker.

TRANSPARENT SOAP/FROST SOAP

This recipe is made in a 3½-quart slow cooker. Don't use this amount in a smaller pot, as it needs headroom. Don't use a larger pot, or it will dry out too much and you won't be able to use the hand blender.

➤ YIELDS 4-8 OUNCES OF FROST SOAP AND 16-20 OUNCES OF TRANSPARENT SOAP ◄

6.5 ounces coconut oil
6.5 ounces palm oil
6.5 ounces castor oil
8.25 ounces water, divided
3 ounces lye

10 ounces (plus 2 ounces more if needed for clarity) 90 percent ethanol (190 proof vodka), at room temperature

5 ounces sugar
Color, fragrances, and other additives as desired

1. Place the coconut oil, palm oil, and castor oil in a 3½-quart slow cooker, turn on high, and put on the lid. If you have a stainless steel easy-read thermometer, you can place it in the pot and lift it out of the melted, warmed oils to check the temperature.

2. When the oils are up to 135°F–140°F, turn the slow cooker down to low. Keep the oils at 130°F–140°F.

3. Place 6.25 ounces water in a heatproof container. Sprinkle the lye onto the water and stir until the lye is dissolved.

4. When the lye solution cools to about 135°F–140°F, pour it slowly into the oils. Stir with a silicone spatula to blend completely.

5. Wearing an oven mitt over your rubber glove, tilt the slow cooker enough so the head of your hand blender is completely submerged. (This prevents air getting whipped into the mixture.)

6. Blend in short pulses, alternately stirring and scraping the sides with the spatula, until the mix has come to medium trace. (This will happen quite quickly.)

7. Put the lid on the slow cooker. (It is important not to open the lid unless you have to. You want to prevent evaporation.)

8. Let the traced soap batter sit in the slow cooker on low with the lid on for 2 hours, or until it is neutral. Stir it once every 30 minutes while it neutralizes to keep the soap batter cooking evenly. The mass may get puffy, but the stirring releases the built-up air.

9. It will get gel-like around the edges after the first 30 minutes. Using the silicone spatula, blend the soap together completely. After another 30 minutes, stir well again, being sure to incorporate any bits that are getting dry on the edges. These need to incorporate back into the mass so they don't show up as flecks later.

10. Cook for another 30 minutes. Stir well, incorporating the dry bits as before.

11. After another 30 minutes, stir well and remove a very small sample of soap with the spatula. Scrape the sample onto a double thickness of paper towel or a paper plate. This will provide you with a disposable testing site. Drip a drop of phenolphthalein on the sample. If it turns vibrant pink, the soap needs more cooking. If it is barely pink to clear, proceed to the next step.

12. When you've determined the soap is neutral, give it another good stir, scraping the sides of the slow cooker and incorporating all the soap into a homogeneous mass.

13. Pour the room-temperature alcohol into the soap in a medium stream. It will harden the soap quite a bit. Stir well with a wooden spoon or mash with a potato masher to break up as many lumps as you can. (The alcohol will evaporate and the fumes are strong, so stand back! You need to be sure that there are no open flames when doing this: Alcohol fumes are highly flammable.)

14. Drizzle the alcohol and soap mixture on the sides of the slow cooker to help dissolve any dried soap that is sticking to the sides.

15. Use the hand blender to further break down the chunks. The slow cooker will still be hot, so be sure to wear an oven mitt as you tip the crock to the side to make a deep enough amount of soap to submerge the head of the blender. You don't need to completely dissolve all the tiny pieces as they'll dissolve while the alcohol-and-soap mixture cooks.

16. After working it with the hand blender, the soap will look opaque and a little foamy. As the soap cooks, it will liquefy into a clear yellow-to-amber liquid. Try to work quickly so that as little alcohol evaporates as possible.

17. Turn the slow cooker to high, put on the lid, and heat it until it foams up. It will happen quickly, and as long as the lid fits well and is heavy, the boiling mixture will stay inside. You can place a large, folded bath towel on top to help weigh down the lid and absorb any escaping mixture.

18. Check the contents after 15 minutes. There will be some foam and chunky bits on the top. Move the foam aside and spoon some of the clear liquid into a small glass. If there are still little chunks of soap, hand blend again until they're all gone.

19. Turn off the heat and let the soap sit with the lid off for about 10 minutes. This will cause some of the foam to reincorporate into the clear soap without foaming back up.

20. Don't try to incorporate all the foam, as it may cloud the soap. You'll use the foam to make pretty soap with a frosty appearance. Just knock down as much as you can with a good spritz of alcohol.

(continued on next page)

21. Prepare the sugar solution by boiling the remaining 2 ounces water in a saucepan on the stove, then adding the sugar. (It will become a very thick syrup.) Stir well, bring back up to a boil and boil for about 30 seconds. Add the hot sugar syrup to the soap mix in the slow cooker, pouring it right from the pan and stirring well the entire time.

22. There will be a considerable layer of bubbles, similar to "scum" when you make jam and jelly. Let this sit on the surface, gently stirring it in. It will dissolve. Scoop out the stubborn bits.

23. Scoop the foam off the surface of the clear soap. This is the "frost soap" part. Put it in a mixing cup (a heatproof glass 4-cup measure works perfectly), and work it well with a wooden spoon to get out as much of the air as you can before putting it in the molds. Add color, fragrance, and other additives as desired. Pack into molds or form into spheres and set aside.

24. There will be clear, golden, fluid soap left in the slow cooker. Remove some of this and place it on a clear plastic lid, like one from a margarine tub. Tip the lid to the side to make a little puddle at the edge of the lid. Put the soap-testing lid in the freezer for 10 minutes.

25. Put the lid on the slow cooker while you're waiting to minimize the layer of hardened soap that forms at the surface. You can gently submerge this "skin" to melt it back into the mass.

26. If the soap sample is clear when you take it from the freezer, proceed to the next step. If the soap sample isn't clear at this time, add another ½ ounce of alcohol. Test again. If it still isn't clear, add another ½ ounce. Test again. Even if it still isn't clear, proceed anyway—you'll have pretty soap with a degree of translucency.

27. After the soap is as clear as it is going to get, pour the soap through a strainer into a 4-cup heatproof glass measuring cup. Let the soap cool to 140°F. (This temperature is relatively kind to essential oils, if you're using them, and it will not cause most fragrance oils to cloud the soap.)

28. You can color and fragrance the entire amount the same and pour into a mold or molds. Or you can pour into individual mixing cups and color and fragrance each one differently.

29. As soon as the soap is poured, get it into the freezer. (Make room in the freezer before you get this far. The more quickly the soap cools, the better, for rapid cooling helps with transparency.) When the soap is firm and cool but not frozen, remove it from the freezer.

Sometimes, no matter what you do, your attempt at transparent soap turns out cloudy or opaque. Although disappointing—since the entire idea of going through all this is to have beautifully transparent soap—don't be discouraged. If your soap isn't transparent, it is still beautiful and extremely useful.

MAKING CREAM SOAP

Cream soapmaking takes a lot of time and a lot of patience. You cook the soap in the slow cooker, let it cool overnight, then whip in extra water with a heavy-duty mixer. You can use your cream soap once it is whipped, but it will improve in texture when aged at least a week. Old-time soapmakers called this "rotting." Essential oils, clay, herbs, and other enhancements can be added before or after rotting.

Making cream soap is the most experimental procedure in the book. There are so many factors that affect the outcome that it will take many batches and long waiting periods before you really get a grip on it. Think of this recipe and procedure as a starting place for much continued experimentation.

CREAM SOAP IN THE SLOW COOKER

This formula makes approximately 38 ounces of soap paste that you will transform into cream soap. It will fit nicely in the 3½-quart slow cooker you've been using.

4 ounces palm stearic acid
5 ounces coconut oil
2 ounces soy oil
3 ounces olive oil
2 ounces castor oil

25 ounces water
1 ounce vegetable glycerin
0.25 ounce sodium hydroxide
    (NaOH)

3 ounces potassium hydroxide
    (KOH)
2–6 ounces additional water,
    added during beating

(continued on next page)

1. Preheat the slow cooker on high.

2. Place the stearic acid, coconut oil, soy oil, olive oil, and castor oil in the slow cooker. Make the lye solution when the oils and stearic acid are melted.

3. Place the water and glycerin in a heatproof container.

4. Sprinkle the sodium hydroxide and potassium hydroxide into the water and stir carefully until dissolved. Don't wait for the solution to cool.

5. Pour the lye solution in a thin stream into the oils, stirring while pouring. (The solution will get white, milky, and possibly grainy.)

6. Blend with an immersion blender until smooth. Wait 5 minutes. If it separates, blend until smooth. Wait 5 minutes and check again. Keep blending and waiting until it stays together.

7. Once it stays smooth, put the lid on the slow cooker.

8. Check every 20 minutes, stirring to make sure it cooks evenly. The texture will change from liquid to lumpy as the cook progresses.

9. After 2½ hours, check for neutrality. Smear a bit of soap on a paper towel. Place a drop of phenolphthalein on the soap. If it turns pink, it's not neutral and needs to cook more. Cook for another 15 minutes and check again. Repeat until the test indicates neutrality.

10. Turn off the cooker and let it sit, covered, overnight.

11. The next day, scoop the soap lumps into the bowl of an electric stand mixer. (A heavy-duty mixer with a paddle or heavy beater is best because it's less likely to whip extra air into the cream soap than thinner blades.) Add 2 ounces of water.

12. With the mixer on the slowest setting, mix the mass until it is smooth. Increase the speed of the mixer and beat the cream soap until it is fluffy, like meringue. If the soap doesn't get as light as you want, add more water, 2 ounces at a time.

13. Place the whipped cream soap in a plastic container with a tight-fitting lid. You can either make additions to it now, or let the soap rot before making additions. Plan on stirring the soap once a day for a week. A lot of the air whipped into the soap will escape as the air bubbles collapse. If the soap is too runny, leave the lid off so that the extra water can evaporate.

When you decide your soap is ready, make additions and package it. Jars, tubes, and airless pumps are ideal for cream soap. The drawback with a jar is that you have to put your hand in it to scoop out the soap, which can increase the chances of spoilage. Look for "tottles," which are tube/bottle hybrids.

Getting the cream soap into containers can be tricky, particularly containers with small openings. Counterintuitively, cream soap just gets thicker and more stubborn when heated, so that won't work like it does for other semi-solids. A pastry tube or a heavy-duty zipper bag with one corner cut off will help you get the cream soap through small openings.

Because the amount of air whipped into your cream soap drastically alters the weight, you'll fill by volume, not weight. The more "whipped" the soap, the less it will weigh. So instead of weighing the amount determined by your container, size up how much to prepare by eye.

Eleven ounces of this cream soap recipe with up to 6 ounces of additional water will fit perfectly in the bowl of a heavy-duty stand mixer.

There are many ways to use cream soap, and these are just a few recipes to get you started. Store the rotted cream soap in the covered plastic container in the refrigerator and remove the amount you need to create each project.

WATCH FOR SPOILAGE

Because of the high water content in cream soap, even after fully "rotting," it may be susceptible to spoilage due to bacteria present in even the cleanest water. Consider using a cosmetic preservative such as Germaben II or Germall. You can find them in the lotion supply section of your soapmaking supplier's website.

OCEAN FRESH CREAM SOAP

YIELDS ENOUGH TO FILL ONE
AIRLESS PUMP, JAR, OR "TOTTLE"

Plain cream soap to fit container
Aqua Flora fragrance oil
Blue food coloring

1. Place the plain cream soap in a small mixing bowl.
2. Add the Aqua Flora fragrance oil and stir well. (Try approximately ¼ teaspoon per 1 ounce of whipped cream soap to start, then adjust after you've used it and made notes.)
3. Add the colorant, drop by drop, incorporating well until you get the desired color. (Add the colorant after the scent material because many fragrance and essential oils have color of their own.)
4. Spoon or squeeze the cream soap into the container.

CHOCOLATE-VANILLA PARFAIT CREAM SOAP

YIELDS ENOUGH TO FILL ONE
AIRLESS PUMP, JAR, OR TUBE

Plain cream soap to fit container
Dutch Chocolate fragrance oil
Special Edition Vanilla fragrance oil
Cocoa powder
Ground vanilla bean powder

1. Divide the plain cream soap between two small mixing bowls.
2. Add the chocolate fragrance oil to one bowl and the vanilla fragrance oil to the other, and stir well. (Try approximately ¼ teaspoon per 1 ounce of whipped cream soap to start, then adjust after you've used it and made notes.)
3. Stir the cocoa powder into the chocolate-scented soap and the vanilla bean powder into the vanilla-scented half. Start with ¼ teaspoon of each.
4. In alternating layers, spoon or squeeze the cream soap into the container.

CHAPTER ELEVEN

HOW TO CAST SOAP

Also known as "melt and pour" or "melt and mold," soap casting is a wonderfully accessible method of making soap at home. A simple meltable soap base, commonly called glycerin soap base, is re-created in a dazzling array of forms. From the simple single pour to the most complicated multipour slices, soap casting is an excellent creative outlet.

MORE THAN JUST MELTING AND POURING

You can buy a bar of glycerin soap at the grocery, bring it home, cut it up, melt it in the microwave, pour it into a little plastic storage container, cool it, pop it out, and have a bar of soap. That is soap casting at its simplest, but it is just the beginning. The soapmaker can manipulate the plain soap base in an incredible variety of ways. Making additions and altering the shape of the soap are the bare bones of the procedures.

Before you begin your soap-casting endeavor, you'll need to estimate the number of ounces of soap needed. To do this, fill the molds with water and pour it off into a graduated glass measuring cup. If you have 2 cups of water, you'll need approximately 1 pound of soap. It is better to over- than underestimate. Have an extra container handy in which to pour the overflow. You can always use it for another project.

CHOOSING A BASE

For many beginning soapmakers, soap casting is a desirable technique because there is no need to use caustics. The soap has been premade with a commercial version of the lye-and-oil method soapmakers use at home. The lye part has already been done for you. Once difficult to find, glycerin soap base is now readily available. You can find many varieties, along with casting supplies, at craft and large fabric stores. Clear glycerin soap from the bar-soap bins in the grocery store works well, too. You need to experiment with bases until you find the kind you like.

What to Look For

When shopping for a base, you need to have some hands-on experience so you can compare. Get some transparent bars at the grocery or 1 pound of each kind offered at the craft store, and do some testing. You're looking for soap that melts easily, has no strong odor, isn't sticky when hardened, doesn't change color under normal conditions, and doesn't "sweat" excessively. Discoloration, stickiness, and odors can happen to good-quality soap base if it is old, has been remelted a number of times, or is exposed to excessively high temperatures. Lower-quality soap base will have these properties right out of the package or after normal use.

WHAT IS SWEATING?

Sweating happens as the glycerin in the soap attracts moisture from the air. Even the best bases will sweat in high humidity. Low-quality bases will sweat all the time. To prevent sweating in general, wrap your hardened casting-soap projects right away and store out of high humidity.

Where to Find It

It pays to get the best base you can, and this usually means shopping for a good base by going to online suppliers where you can find high-quality casting soap at reasonable prices. However, not all bases found on the Internet are of high quality. Ask around and ask for samples or purchase small amounts.

SOAP-CASTING EQUIPMENT

In some cases, convenience is the most important thing in choosing soapmaking supplies. An easy-read thermometer from the grocery store is going to be the same easy-read thermometer from the soap supply specialist. A lot of the equipment you will need for soap casting can be found in your average big-box department store, or even the supermarket. Check out your local stores to find the best value.

Double Boiler

The casting-soap artisan's best friend is a stainless steel double boiler with a lid. You can improvise a double boiler by using a metal bowl over a saucepan. You can even do some projects using heatproof heavy glass measuring cups. However, a good double boiler set will make your life much easier and your soap much better.

SOAP-CASTING THERMOMETER

You will need an instant-read thermometer. There are many instances in soap casting where the accurate measure of temperature is essential. Get two, as you may need to measure the temperatures of two containers at the same time.

You can still use your double boiler for food after you've used it for soap casting. Just be sure it's thoroughly clean. Even a minuscule bit of soap can make food taste funny. It's not enough to make you sick; it's just not at all delicious.

Scale

As in lye soapmaking, you'll need a scale. Since the chemistry is already done for you, you don't need to have as accurate a scale as you do for lye soapmaking. You should, however, get the best scale you can afford, both for accuracy and because it is likely you will need it when you make cold- and hot-process soap.

Alcohol

Rubbing alcohol in a spray bottle is a simple and essential tool. A spritz of alcohol will eliminate the bubbles that rise to the surface of the soap after pouring. It will also help you prepare the surface of cooled soap and embeddable objects to adhere to a second pour.

If you also make transparent soap using the hot-process method, you'll have ethanol on hand, and that will work perfectly in all soap-casting applications in a pinch, but rubbing alcohol is much less expensive and it's easy to get.

MOLDS FOR SOAP CASTING

One of the most exciting parts of soap casting is choosing your molds. Here are a few of the different options. (Tube molds are a special type of mold, with their own techniques, which will be described in the next section.)

Block Molds

Some techniques use block molds. The big block of soap that comes out of such a mold will be sliced into bars. You will also use block molds when making soap of contrasting colors to combine in other projects.

If the molded shape isn't important to your project, you can use pretty much anything as a block mold. Most serving-ware containers do very well. Keep in mind that you will see all the details of the container in your end product, so you'll have bumps, curves, mold marks, and lines in your bars. Those can be a pleasing part of the handmade soap experience. You can, of course, trim the odd bits with a dough scraper, paring knife, or cheese plane.

You can buy domed or "log" block molds created especially for soap-casting projects that are meant to be sliced like loaves. You can also use a plastic-lined or stainless steel baking loaf mold. These are great for multistage pours where you pour some, place some, pour some more, then cool and slice.

Bar Molds

Bar molds can be simple rectangles or exquisite carvings transformed into vessels for creating beautiful soaps. You can find a growing number of suitable molds at craft and some mass-market stores. The Internet is an invaluable resource, as you can find molds that are sturdier and of a wider variety.

Generally, your casting soap will readily release from a bar mold. If it's a little stubborn, you can put it in the freezer for about 10 minutes. The soap will contract and pull away from the sides of the molds, making for easier release. Some soapmakers use a silicone or cooking spray, but this isn't usually needed.

Improvised Molds

You can forage in your kitchen for all kinds of interesting molds, such as ice-cube trays and plastic gelatin molds. Don't forget the recycling bin. The bumpy bottoms of plastic soda bottles make very interesting shapes. Cut the molded shape away from the rest of the plastic with heavy kitchen shears. Be sure to protect your hands as the edges can be sharp.

Molds made from heavier gauge plastic will last considerably longer, but they still need to be well cared for. Any mold will eventually crack after repeated use, but if you take good care of them, your molds will help you make beautiful soap for a long time, batch after batch.

Tray Molds and Beyond

A tray mold is a single-cavity mold with score marks for guidance in cutting your soap into bars after unmolding. Some have designs, too, such as lavender stems and animal figures. These are a beautiful hybrid of bar and block molds.

There are various three-dimensional molds available, as well. You can use two-part molds that you fasten together, seal, and pour. When the soap is hard, you take off the clips and release the form. You'll need to clean off the mold lines for a finished look. There are also flexible vinyl molds that you pull away from the sides and top, and silicone molds that you stretch and peel off the hardened soap.

USING TUBE MOLDS

One of the most exciting ways to add detail to soap-casting projects is through embedding shapes from a tube mold. Tube molds are just that—long tubes—and they are available in a variety of shapes. You pour the tube full, let the soap inside harden, then push it out. You have a long piece of soap that you can embed whole or cut into pieces.

Use small pipe to make thin rods of soap, larger ones for bigger rods. These also work well for making round bars. You just push out the hard soap and slice! Freezing the soap in the tube makes removal easier.

Some of the simplest tube molds are made from PVC pipe. You can buy PVC at hardware stores and have it cut to length. Buy the caps that fit the ends so you won't have to worry about how you're going to seal the mold. Get the threaded, screw-on caps if you can, as they're the easiest to remove.

You can find stainless steel tubes in animal and geometric shapes at cake decorating stores. They are intended for baking bread into fancy shapes for canapés. You just pour the soap in instead, and you've got a star, a heart, a duck, or one of many other shapes.

More and more soap mold companies are making tube molds, which are sometimes called vertical molds. Some are in two pieces and clamped together. This is for ease of removal; you just unclamp and pull the two halves of the mold free. Other companies make simple one-piece tubes that you need to seal yourself.

Most of the time you spend with this kind of mold is in prepping the mold and getting the soap out of it. You usually make tubes of soap as part of another project, so having a storage container for the specific project at hand is a good idea. You may, of course, also use the tubes as finished soaps.

You need to determine the number of ounces of soap you'll need for the tube mold you're using. For this first recipe, use a 1" diameter PVC pipe cut to 12" long. You should be able to buy an end cap where you buy the pipe, but if you can't find one, use heavy plastic wrap and rubber bands to seal the end. Pieces cut from heavy freezer bags or heavy painting tarps work well. Be sure to keep the end of the mold in a container when you pour, in case the seal gives way.

UNMOLDING A TUBE MOLD

Getting the soap out of a tube mold can be frustrating. You will probably have to freeze the soap for a while, after it's hard, to get it out of the mold. Take the mold out of the freezer after about an hour. Let it sit on the counter until condensation forms on the plastic mold. Take off the seal and push firmly with your fingers, a broom handle, a plunger made from a disk of wood and a stick, or you can invest in a pressurized air system. It will take some practice, but you'll eventually find a way to get the soap out. If you don't use tubes often, you won't mind the struggle, but if you do it a lot, you'll need a good system.

Another method of sealing a mold involves pouring a little puddle of casting soap on the work surface and setting the mold in it so that as the soap hardens it will hold it in place. This works best with molds that would stand up on their own anyway. Tall, heavy molds will tip over, breaking the seal and making a mess.

After you've sealed one end of the tube mold, fill it with water to test it before committing to melted soap. If the water leaks out, you need to readjust the seal. Pour the water into a graduated measuring cup to see how much soap you need to melt.

It is a good idea to support the tube molds upright in a pitcher or other tall container that won't be easily knocked over while the soap is hardening. A small box padded with a towel that can be shaped to hold the mold upright is a simple solution. Or for one thin mold like the one in the recipe that follows, a plastic pitcher and a hand towel should work well. Roll the towel and place it into the pitcher. Make an opening in the center of the roll for the mold to slip into. If there is too much room, use another towel.

CLEAN SMART

Never rinse large blobs of soap, either finished or unsaponified, down your drains. They will clog up almost immediately. Instead, use smart cleanup techniques. Wipe extra soap off tools and scrape it out of the pan. When you're done, rinse everything with hot water. If you've used oils as additives to your casting project, you may need to use a little regular dish detergent.

Let the soap sit until it is back to room temperature and store it in a way appropriate for the project you're going to use it in. If you're going to use the soap as-is, cut it into little disks or round bars.

 BASIC TUBE MOLD

| 12 ounces clear soap base | 2–3 drops soap colorant (or more as desired) | Pinch mica |
| | | 1 teaspoon soap fragrance |

1. Fill the bottom pan of the double boiler with water, put on the top pan, and turn the heat on high.

2. Cut the soap base into approximately 1" cubes. Place in the top pan. Add two drops of colorant, the mica, and the fragrance. Put on the lid.

3. When the water in the bottom pan comes to a boil, turn off the heat and remove the pan from the heat. Let sit for 15–20 minutes. Take off the lid. (The soap should all be melted.) Gently stir to combine the mica and colorant. Check for color. If you want deeper color, add more colorant a drop at a time.

4. Take the top pan off and wipe the condensation off the bottom so that it does not fall into the mold. Place the tube mold upright in the towel in the pitcher; be sure the bottom is sealed. Fill the mold. Set aside to cool. After about an hour, place the tube mold in the freezer for another hour. Remove it, let it sit until condensation forms, remove the seal, and push the soap out of the mold. Store as desired or cut into disks or tube-shaped bars.

CHAPTER TWELVE

SOAP-CASTING PROJECTS

Now it's time to explore the fullness of the creativity you can express through the medium of casting soap. From a simple swirl of sparkle encased in transparent soap to elaborate, hand-formed geodes and gems, you will find endless expressions for your ideas. Practice the basics, then build them into each other to create the soap of your dreams.

SINGLE POUR IN BLOCKS

This is the basic technique you'll use to expand your repertoire. It doesn't get any simpler than this. But that doesn't mean it has to be boring!

These recipes are formulated using 1 pound of soap as the basic unit. You can, of course, make more, but 1-pound batches are a good place to start. You can slice them into bars or cut them into shapes you'll use in other projects.

For single pours, you need to find a block mold that will hold the amount of soap you're working with. Your best bet is plastic storage ware. It needs to be heat resistant, flexible, and of a dimension that will make it easy to cut bars into the size you want.

Longer, deeper molds can be used as "loaf" molds. Square, shallow molds create a squared shape that you can cut into bars as you'd cut brownies. If you are pouring soap to be used as strips, chunks, or other pieces to be embedded in another pour, you need to be sure the mass you create will provide you with the shapes and sizes you need.

To check the volume of a mold, fill it with water. Then pour the water into a measuring cup to see how much there is. Adjust your recipe to fit your mold, or use another mold.

BASIC 3-INGREDIENT BLOCK SOAP

1 pound clear soap base

2–5 drops colorant

1 teaspoon fragrance oil or
essential oil

Rubbing alcohol

1. Cut the casting soap into approximately 1" cubes. Place the soap in the top of a double boiler or a 4-cup heatproof glass measuring cup. Add 2 drops of colorant, and see if you like the way it looks. Add more if you want. If you're using fragrance oil, add it now. If you're using essential oil, wait until the soap is ready to pour.

2. Place water in the bottom of the double boiler. Put on the top pan. Heat the water until it boils. Cover the pan with the lid. Remove from the heat. Let it sit undisturbed for 30 minutes. Check the soap. After it's melted, stir the soap gently with a rubber scraper. (Avoid too much stirring action so you won't get bubbles.) If you're using essential oil, add it now.

3. Pour the melted soap into the mold, taking care to pour from a short distance so you don't make bubbles or splash. You will get some bubbles, and you can get rid of them with a spritz of alcohol. (Be sure not to spray the alcohol near the heated burner or open flame.)

4. Let the soap cool and harden for about 1 hour. (It could take more or less time depending on the temperature of the room.) If you're in a hurry, you can place the mold in the freezer to speed up the cooling and solidifying; just make sure you don't forget that it's in there. Completely freezing the soap can cause it to "sweat" after it returns to room temperature.

Single Pour Variations

For each of the recipes that follow, use the same basic steps as for the Basic 3-Ingredient Block Soap recipe in this chapter.

LAVENDER OAT FLOAT

Add the oats and lavender and stir well. The oats and lavender will float on the surface of the soap, making a scrubby layer.

1 pound casting soap
1 teaspoon lavender essential oil

2 tablespoons rolled oats, gently pulsed in a coffee grinder, but not powdered

1 tablespoon dried lavender flowers

A BIT OF THE SEA

Nori is dried seaweed, used, among other things, in making sushi. You can break up solid sheets, which may be easier to find. You can get a variety of nori products in Asian food stores or the Asian foods section of your grocery store.

1 pound casting soap
Pinch sea blue mica
Pinch sea green mica
1 teaspoon Ocean fragrance oil

SEAWEED SALT SCRUB

1 pound casting soap
4 drops blue food coloring
1 teaspoon Spa fragrance oil
Coarse sea salt, or regular coarse salt
Nori shreds or flakes

1. Place the soap in the top of a double boiler and place water in the bottom. Heat the water and melt the soap. Add the food coloring and fragrance oil.

2. Pour it into the mold, and immediately sprinkle the salt evenly over the surface of the soap. (It will sink, forming a layer at the bottom of the mold.)

3. When the soap has cooled a little, sprinkle the nori flakes on top in an even layer. Let cool and slice into chunks for a great home-spa salt scrub!

BLOCK OVER-POURS

In the 1990s, an exciting trend in soap began appearing in shops in Southern California: fanciful bars of transparent soap containing pieces of contrasting soap. Beautiful compositions of color, shape, and scent brought handcrafted soap to a new height of popularity.

Of course, these pay homage to Catherine Failor and her early experiments with placing colorful transparent soap inside opaque cold-process soap. When you combine your imagination, tastes, and personal style, you will create highly original designs.

To get you started, here are some projects organized around general thematic material. You can make one or all of them, or just use these ideas as inspiration for your own creations:

- **Serenity:** Wavy lines, a monochromatic color scheme, and a soft, oceany scent blend together to create serenity in a bar of soap.

- **Natural girls:** Pink kid-silhouettes, oatmeal, and lavender combine to make a scrubby soap fit for your best friend.

- **Shining star:** A silvery star embedded in a glittery, deep blue background scented with a dreamy fragrance.

- **Bath duck:** White soap with a yellow ducky in the middle.

- **Mosaic window:** Silver soap poured around "panes" of jewel-toned soap creates an image of glowing beauty.

Although you will probably want to make your own embeddables, you can also buy them premade where you buy other soapmaking supplies. There are curls, shreds, shapes, figures, and all kinds of other premade soap pieces to save you a step in creating combinations like those in the list.

BAR OVER-POURS

If an intricate mold can be enhanced with a simple pour, so can a simple mold be enhanced with an over-pour. And for a soap with extra visual excitement, do over-pours in a fancy mold! To create these effects, you pour a lightly tinted base over pieces in one or more colors.

Leaf Domes for All Seasons

For these projects, you will need two different molds: a three-cavity dome mold and a small leaf tray mold in assorted shapes.

 # SPRING

12 ounces casting soap
Medium green colorant
Scent of your choice
Light green colorant
Pale green colorant
Light green mica
Rubbing alcohol

1. Prepare ahead a 3-ounce casting soap, tinted medium green and scented, and a 3-ounce casting soap, tinted light green and scented. Pour these into leaf molds, allowing at least two leaves for each dome mold. Let harden and unmold.

2. Place 2 green casting soap leaves into each dome mold.

3. Melt the remaining 6 ounces of casting soap, scent and tint with 1 drop of pale green colorant and 1 pinch of light green mica for the over-pour. Spritz the leaves with alcohol.

4. Cool the over-pour to 125°F and pour over the leaves. Adjust with a chopstick as needed.

5. Let harden and unmold. Wrap in plastic film.

 # FALL

12 ounces casting soap
Medium orange colorant
Fall Foliage fragrance oil from Sweet Cakes
Golden yellow colorant
Pale orange colorant
Gold mica
Rubbing alcohol

1. Prepare ahead a 3-ounce casting soap, tinted medium orange and scented, and a 3-ounce casting soap, tinted golden yellow and scented. Pour these into leaf molds, allowing at least 2 leaves for each dome mold. Let harden and unmold.

2. Place 2 leaves in each dome mold.

3. Melt the remaining 6 ounces of casting soap, scent and tint with 1 drop of pale orange colorant and a pinch of gold mica for the over-pour. Spritz the leaves with alcohol.

4. Cool the over-pour to 125°F and pour over the leaves. Adjust with a chopstick as needed.

5. Let harden and unmold. Wrap in plastic film.

GOURMET CHOCOLATE SHELLS

For this project you will need a 1-ounce shell mold and a 4-ounce oval dome mold.
Techniques used include color swirling in the mold, layering, and over-pour.

4 ounces casting soap cut into small pieces
7 drops cloudy white gel colorant from TKB Trading

3 drops Chocolate Raisin colorant from TKB Trading
Rubbing alcohol

¼ teaspoon Dutch Chocolate fragrance oil from Symphony Scents
¹/8 teaspoon iridescent gold soap-safe glitter

1. Melt ½ ounce of the soap and add 2 drops of the cloudy white gel colorant. Hold the shell mold at an angle and pour ¼ of the soap into the mold. Let cool.

2. Melt another ½ ounce soap and add Chocolate Raisin colorant. Spritz the surface of the partially filled shell with alcohol, and, holding the shell at a different slant, pour in another ¼ of the soap. Repeat this process two more times, alternating the white and chocolate colors and turning and slanting the tiny mold as you go for a randomly layered effect. Cool the shell. Remove from the mold.

3. Place the finished shell in the bottom of the oval dome mold with the detail side touching the bottom of the mold.

4. Melt the remaining 3 ounces of soap. Scent with the Dutch Chocolate fragrance oil. When the soap cools to 120°F, sprinkle the glitter into the soap and pour enough of the soap into the oval dome mold to come up even with the back of the shell. Spritz with alcohol. Let sit until there is a skin on the first pour.

5. Add the remaining 5 drops of cloudy white gel colorant. Reheat to 120°F if needed. Pour over the shell and first pour. Let sit until firm. Remove from the mold and wrap in plastic wrap.

EMBEDS

You can embed nearly anything in a bar of soap. Plastic bugs and goldfish, silk flowers, semiprecious stones, and rubber ducks can all be completely or partially encased in soap for an effect that ranges from the silly to the sublime. Just be sure the embedded object is something you'd actually enjoy finding in your soap!

A Few Words from the Embed Expert

Kerith Henderson of Pisces Soap in Hollywood, California, is one of the most inventive soapmakers using this technique. Her designs, from the sweet and whimsical to the strictly bizarre, are fresh and innovative. Here are her top five tips for beginners:

1. Get creative. Don't think that you have to create the same soap bars that everyone else is doing. Don't be afraid to express yourself.
2. Don't let failure discourage you if a recipe you try turns out wrong. Learning from your mistakes is the best soapmaking lesson you can get.
3. Start off small. In the beginning, you don't have to run out and purchase every fancy oil, fragrance, herb, and additive out there. Start with the basics while you are still getting the techniques down.
4. Do your research. Spend as much time as possible reading every book and newsletter you can get your hands on. If you have access to the Internet, join a couple of soapmaking newsgroups where you can learn and share with others.
5. Enjoy yourself. Soapmaking can be a tremendous amount of fun and a huge stress release. So get to it and have a ball!

Have a child who hates to take baths? She will soon be begging to stay in the tub once she gets a hold of these soap bars! Soaps embedded with plastic toys add whimsy and fun to everyday bathing.

KERITH HENDERSON'S EMBEDDED TOY SOAPS

Make sure the toys you use are made of a softer plastic or vinyl. Hard toys can scrape delicate skin! Squeak toys, rubber balls, erasers, and soft plastic insects are great choices. Don't forget: The toys must fit in the molds you choose!

Casting soap cut into small pieces and melted
Small toy
Rubbing alcohol

1. Pour melted soap into your mold, about ¼ of the way full. Allow this to cool slightly, forming a thin skin.

2. Spritz the selected toy bottom with rubbing alcohol. Place the toy into the soap, breaking the thin skin. Allow this layer to set. (This bottom layer is what keeps the toy from floating to the top!)

3. Generously spritz the toy and bottom layer with rubbing alcohol. Pour the rest of the melted soap in to fill the mold. Let the soap set completely before popping it out of the mold.

EMBEDDED FLOWER SOAP

The hardest part of this project is keeping the air bubbles on the flowers to a minimum. The alcohol will help with this, but if there are air bubbles remaining, don't worry. They will look like dewdrops on the petals. You need a mold deep enough and big enough to hold the flower head. These projects look best with soap that is either uncolored or very slightly tinted. The color of the flower will reflect and be magnified in the soap, so you don't need any additional color.

Flat silk flowers, such as daisies
Casting soap cut into small pieces
Rubbing alcohol

1. Pull off the head of the flower and cut off any sharp plastic part on the back. Rinse the flower in very warm water to release any dyes that are not colorfast. Let the flower head dry.

2. Place the prepared flower into the mold, pretty side down.

3. Melt the soap. When the soap reaches 140°F, carefully pour it around the flower—do not pour directly onto the flower. As you pour, gently agitate the mold to release air bubbles. Use a chopstick or bamboo skewer to poke air pockets from between the petals. As the bubbles rise, spritz with alcohol to get rid of them. Allow the soap to cool, and unmold.

MULTISTAGE POURS

With a bit of patience and practice, you can create amazingly complex yet beautifully simple-to-make layered melt-and-pour soaps. You can layer in a block mold or in a bar mold, or combine both. You are limited only by your patience.

~ KERITH HENDERSON'S LAYERED SOAP BARS ~

1. Pour your first layer of soap. Let it cool so that a thick layer of skin forms on top. (You don't want the entire layer to be hardened, just the top skin.)

2. Spritz the first layer generously with rubbing alcohol. (Alcohol poured into a spritz bottle works best. Rubbing alcohol primes this first layer, allowing the next layer to stick.)

3. Pour your second layer. If you only want two layers, allow your soap to cool completely before taking it out of the mold. If you would like to add more than two layers of color, repeat steps 1 and 2 until you achieve the desired effect.

Soothing Spiral

This bar, made with a mold with a spiral inscribed in it, created in silver and blue mica with a relaxing ocean scent, can conjure serenity through its relaxing colors and scent.

Melt a tiny amount of soap, color with a sparkly silver colorant and pour into the spiral only. Wipe up any extra soap. When the spiral has set, melt enough soap to fill the mold. Tint it transparent blue with blue soap colorant. Scent with an oceany scent. Fill the mold with the transparent blue.

Sassy Spiral

That same mold shape can take on an entirely different attitude when crafted with a neon pink spiral on an electric blue base. Using the same mold as the previous design, this soap will give you a burst of energy from the neon color and the fun, fruity scent.

Melt a tiny amount of soap, color with pink neon colorant, and pour into the spiral only. Wipe up any extra soap. When the spiral has set, melt enough soap to fill the mold. Tint it with neon blue soap colorant. Scent with a fun berry scent. Fill the mold with the neon blue soap.

Cameo Technique

To achieve an old-fashioned cameo-like effect, coat the inside of a relief design with a thin layer of white soap. The relief part of the design is the part that will look raised or inset on the surface of the finished soap. Let this accent cool completely, then pour the second layer with the appropriate background color. Since the first layer is so thin, you may find it helpful to chill it before the second pour.

GEODES

This is a great project to use up all those casting soap scraps you've been accumulating. Or you can, of course, make soap especially for this project. To form the geodes, you will chop casting soap into two sizes. You'll tint the little chunks and form them into spheres of two layers. Then you'll dip-coat them with darkly colored soap. This is a very messy project, so you may want to wear latex gloves.

GEODE SOAP

Beware of unintentional visual effects. For example, a geode with a yellow core and sparkly white second layer might sound pretty, but upon opening it you may discover you have created something that looks like a hard-boiled egg!

7 ounces casting soap
15 drops fragrance oil or essential oil

Mica color
Dark colorant
Very warm water

Melted untinted soap (optional)

1. Divide 4 ounces of the casting soap into two equal pieces. Chop one piece very finely, about the size of diced onions. Then chop the other piece into larger chunks of about ¼" to ⅓" square.

2. Drop about 5 drops of fragrance oil or essential oil onto the first pile of smaller chunks. (This is the crystal center of the geode.) Work the fragrance in with your fingers and start packing the pieces into a ball. Press it firmly together, compacting it as much as you can.

3. Sprinkle the second pile, the larger chunks, with the mica color of your choice. Gently toss the chunks to coat. Add about 10 drops of fragrance oil or essential oil and work it into the pieces, then pack these pieces around the crystal center. (A good way to do this is to put about ⅓ of the pile on one hand, pressing it tightly with the other hand.) Repeat until you have pressed all of the larger chunks very tightly around the firmly packed center. Set this tightly packed core aside.

4. Melt the remaining 3 ounces of casting soap in a 1-cup heatproof glass measuring cup and add enough dark colorant to make it nearly black or dark brown. Let it cool to about 120°F.

5. Place the core in the cup of melted dark soap and turn it to coat it. Using a stainless steel serving spoon, remove the ball and place it on a piece of aluminum foil. Let the surface harden, then repeat, dipping and cooling in the same way. Repeat until there is a complete, thin layer of dark soap coating the entire surface. Let cool completely.

6. Fill a tall water glass with the warm water. Dip a nonserrated table knife in the water to warm it. Grasp the soap sphere firmly with one hand and carefully and very quickly slice through it with the knife.

7. Gently separate the halves. Wow! What a beautiful geode! If you wish, you can coat the cut surface with untinted melted soap. Wrap the halves in clear plastic. They may crumble in use, but that won't matter because they're so beautiful!

SOAP GEMS

One of the most exciting artists working in melt-and-pour soap is RuthAnn Wachsmuth of Mermaid's Bath. She is a stay-at-home mother of two, talented artist, and visionary in micro-business bath and body. Her soap gems are much sought-after, and she agreed to share some of her specialized techniques for creating incredibly beautiful "stones" from casting soap. Here are RuthAnn's top ten tips:

1. Do your research before jumping in. Just because it's the "latest thing" doesn't mean you can sell it to your client base.
2. Make the best product you can.
3. Think about your packaging. You could make the best soap in the world, but if the label doesn't catch the customer's eye, they'll never know.
4. Charge fairly for it; there will always be cheaper soap. Make sure your clients appreciate how special yours is.
5. Get the best ingredients you can afford. Inferior ingredients produce inferior products.
6. Keep careful notes on each batch. An unnoted tweak might turn out something exquisite that you won't be able to reproduce.
7. Don't do it for the money. If you are just looking to make a quick buck, it's not in soap.
8. Educate yourself. Don't expect others to instantly share *all* their secrets they worked on just because you are a newbie. They worked hard for that knowledge; you should, too.
9. Be willing to share what you learn with others.
10. Enjoy it. If soapmaking becomes drudgery, your product will suffer.

Gemstone Soap: A Brief Tutorial

RuthAnn Wachsmuth has the following advice for gemstone soapmakers:

The first step is to choose a gemstone to recreate in soap. Study the stone—its colors, patterns, how it catches the light. Decide how you want to produce it—just a single soap? In that case, I'd use a large disposable cup. Since I make the stones in quantity, I use a large silicone loaf mold. On fragrance: Obviously, you can scent however you choose. I use a blend of essential oils and scent all batches the same. That way, I can use the trimming from one batch for the next.

I'll use amethyst for my example, since it's one of the first I tried, and a bestseller.

The first thing to make is the base color that will be used for the major chunks of color. In this case, it's a deep purple. After melting the glycerin soap base, add your fragrance and color. I typically use micas to color my soaps, as dyes tend to bleed. Pour into whatever container you have handy. I use small Rubbermaid-type containers.

Once the dark shade has cooled and solidified completely, remove from the mold and chop in haphazard chunks. I usually bang them around a bit to soften the edges. Place three-quarters of the chunks into your mold and melt down the rest. Spritz alcohol on the soap chunks in the mold. Pour the melted soap over the chunks and toss around to get them all coated; make sure they are uneven—not lying in a perfect smooth layer. You want pieces poking up. I often hit them with a little mica to create inclusions. Metallic gold or copper is nice. I have an awesome iridescent blue I'll throw in generously at this point. Give the chunks a poke, allowing the still fluid soap to flow around a bit. Sometimes I prop up the mold at an angle; you want to avoid having a straight line of demarcation between your colors. While I'm poking things around, I melt the next over-pour, which is typically a light version of the first shade.

Spritz your first layer with alcohol, and then pour your second color. Poke around some more. Let it form a skin, dig around, throw in more mica, some fine shards of clear soap and then let set while you melt the next pour.

I use clear with just a little yellow added. Spritz with alcohol; pour the clear. Really dig around. The previous layer should still be soft at this point and you can get some nice color blends and swirls this way. That's about it for the amethyst. For some stones (aquamarine, citrines, opals), I often do a final pour of white to simulate the matrix the stones form in. I often add some bronze mica to the white matrix after it's set for a while and become thickened. The goal there is to create pockets of color, not to tint the entire layer.

Let cool and solidify completely—usually overnight for me.

Unmold and get a big knife. Cut off any curved edges and, if using a large mold, cut into large (palm-sized) chunks for big stones, smaller for more petite stones. Now, begin cutting to look like a roughly mined gemstone. I cut at various angles and bevel edges to create a faceted look. The appearance of the stone will help guide you.

CHAPTER THIRTEEN

HOW TO HAND MILL YOUR SOAP

With the hand-milling technique, you can use either cold-process or hot-process soap. You grate it, heat it, mix in chosen additives, scoop the mixture into molds, and let it set. Soap projects that start out with the intent to use this technique are most often called hand milled.

TYPE OF SOAP TO USE

Thanks to the innovators at soap supply companies, you can purchase ready-made cold-process soap and craft beautiful hand-milling projects without using the lye yourself. You can buy the soap in blocks or bars and shred it yourself. You can also buy preshredded soap from a number of companies. This differs from buying meltable soap for casting soap projects in that the soap is opaque cold-process soap. You may also use hot-process soap.

You can, of course, make your own cold- and hot-process soaps and finish them in this way. You can use completely plain soap, or you can plan a hand-milling project around a batch of soap especially created for the particular project. Or you can use up all those soap scraps you've been saving!

WASTE NOT, WANT NOT

Cleanup after hand milling is similar to cleaning up after casting soap, but you should have incorporated nearly every bit of soap into your recipe. Use the tiny bits of leftover hand-milled soap to wash up the equipment. If the soap is rich and leaves a little film, a good squirt of detergent and some more hot water will finish the cleanup in no time.

You can find soap in health food and grocery stores that is suitable for hand milling. If you decide to try regular commercial bar soap, look for bars that are actually soap. They will have ingredients like sodium tallowate, which is tallow soap, or sodium cocoate, which is coconut oil soap. If a bar says "cleansing bar" or "beauty bar," it is probably not soap, and it won't work at all in your hand-milling projects.

ADVANTAGES OF HAND MILLING

One of the advantages of this method is that you don't subject your additives to the rigors of active lye. You can achieve more predictable color results. Botanicals will hold color longer, and you can use less fragrance material. And, of course, you don't have to handle the lye.

You can get beautifully textured soaps by incorporating dried herbs right in with the soap as you heat it. If you make soap balls by moistening the shreds and packing them by hand rather than melting the soap, the herbs will retain more color. Remember that the herbs will still turn brown before too long, but the change will not be as fast this way.

Since subjecting essential oils to the lye process can diminish their impact per ounce, combining them with the soap shreds can make them go further. The rate of essential oil use in lye soapmaking is approximately 1 tablespoon per pound of fats. However, in hand milling, you can use only 1 *teaspoon* per pound of soap and get a great effect.

HAND-MILLING EQUIPMENT

Much of the equipment you need to make hand-milled soap is the same as for other soapmaking techniques. But you'll also need a few other items, including graters, food processor, double boiler, slow cooker, microwave oven, spoons, scrapers, bowls, molds, and scoops.

Graters

The first thing you need to do in hand-milling is shred your soap. Of course, if you want, you can buy soap already shredded, which will save you a step. But this will limit your options. You need to look at what kinds of shredded soap are available. If you can't find the kind of soap you want already shredded, you can probably find it in blocks, so you'll need to shred it yourself.

To shred blocks of soap, you can use a simple cheese grater and elbow grease. Some soaps are harder to shred than others, so the amount of strength needed will vary. Be sure to take care you don't grate your knuckles as you work.

Use a grating surface that has the larger, approximately ¼", holes. The tiny holes will take forever and produce soap powder, not shreds. (If you want to make soap powder, make shreds first, and when they're very dry, pulverize them in a food processor or with a mortar and pestle.)

Here's how to shred your soap: Hold the grater firmly over a container. Wear heavy-duty gloves or an oven mitt on your hand holding the soap. Draw the surface of the soap over the surface of the grater, using even pressure. The soap may start to collapse as the bar gets smaller. If this happens, just roll it into a ball and keep shredding until there is no more surface area. You can use any stainless steel tool for food again after you've used it for soap, once you've thoroughly cleaned it. If you use them a lot though, consider having some tools just for soaping.

Food Processor

A much faster way to shred your soap is to run the bars through a food processor. You need to be sure your processor has a heavy-duty motor and enough room in the work bowl to accommodate the shreds without compacting them. Select the grating blade with the larger holes. Push the soap through the feed-tube as you would cheese.

Double Boiler

You will need something in which to melt the soap shreds. Many soapers swear by slow cookers, while others wouldn't think of hand milling without a microwave oven. However, the most common method is with a double boiler. To use the double boiler, you place the shreds and the liquid in the top of the boiler, place water in the bottom, heat the water to boiling, and then turn the heat down to simmer. As the soap melts, you add scent and texture materials. You must watch carefully so the boiler doesn't boil dry!

Slow Cooker

With the slow cooker, the process is not unlike making a rich stew. You place the shreds, liquid, and color in the pot, turn it on, and wait for the low, steady heat to do the work. You can use the same slow cooker for hot-process and hand-milling techniques.

You need to watch the level of water. Soap can scorch if it gets too hot without enough water. If you find that your slow cooker dries out the soap mass, increase the amount of water in the recipe at the outset.

You can find inexpensive slow cookers at mass market and thrift stores. It's best if you get one with variable temperature settings. If you buy a used one, be sure that the liner is free of cracks and strange odors.

Microwave Oven

Another way to work with soap shreds is with a microwave oven. This method can be faster than the others, but it can also result in extremely hot melted soap, froth, and hot steam. It is best for small recipes, 1 pound of shreds or less.

If you decide to make larger batches in the microwave, be very careful of the heat. Even the sturdiest plastic can melt under the intensity of the heat. There are very few sheet molds that can stand up to the temperatures, so let it cool before risking your favorites.

Spoons, Scrapers, and Bowls

Whichever heating method you use, you will need other tools just as you have for the other soapmaking methods. As always, use only silicone; thick, heat-safe glass; and stainless steel. Although the soap will not be caustic when you get it for milling, it's still best to use nonreactive tools.

One-piece silicone scrapers with heads that are curved like a scoop are perfect. Get a couple of sizes for big and small tasks. Be sure to watch how they age—as they eventually will—because you don't want chunks of decaying scraper in the soap.

For mixing, a large stainless steel slotted spoon works perfectly. Be sure you have one that has a plastic or rubber covering on the handle rather than naked stainless steel all the way to the end. Plain stainless steel will get too hot to hold.

Molds and Scoops

Make sure your plastic molds are heat resistant. They need to be able to stand up to boiling water. Test the molds with boiling water, as discussed before. You can easily ruin a good plastic mold with too-hot hand-milled soap, especially if you're melting it in the microwave.

TEXTURE OF HAND-MILLED SOAPS

The texture of hand-milled soap will be slightly to very uneven. If you cut it into bars, you will probably get some warping on the sides and edges as the added water evaporates. This shouldn't be seen as a flaw, but as yet another hallmark of having been made by hand.

Scoops are handy to make very pretty soap balls. Scrape the finished soap mass into a block mold. Then, when it's cooled but not totally hard, use a stainless steel ice cream scoop to scoop out portions. Wear latex gloves to protect your hands and always be careful of the heat.

SAMPLE HAND-MILLING RECIPES

Here are simple recipes you can use to practice, one for each of the melting techniques—double boiler, slow cooker, and microwave. Experiment with them and combine elements of different ones until you come up with the method that is right for you.

BASIC HAND-MILLING RECIPE, DOUBLE BOILER METHOD

1 pound shredded, plain cold- or hot-process soap, or 1 pound premade soap shreds

4 ounces water
3–6 drops food coloring
1 teaspoon dried herbs

1 teaspoon fragrance oil or essential oil

1. Place the shreds in the top of a double boiler. Cover. Add the water and the food coloring. Place water in the bottom of the double boiler. Heat the water to boiling, and then turn down to simmer. Stir gently. (Avoid vigorous stirring to keep the foam level to a minimum.)

2. Cover and cook for about 10 minutes. *Don't let the boiler boil dry!* Check the soap mass. It should have started to soften, and even become translucent by now. If it hasn't, just be patient; it will. Stir gently.

3. While the soap mass is heating, set out the rest of the ingredients. Check your soap every 10 minutes or so and keep adding water to the boiler if necessary. When the soap has taken on a translucent look and you can stir the water all the way through, you are ready to make the additions. Sprinkle the herbs over the mass and stir until evenly distributed.

4. Remove ⅓ cup of the soap mass and place it in a warmed glass bowl. Stir the fragrance material into this and then return it to the pan and stir it in thoroughly. If you want to alter the amounts of additives, make further additions and stir well.

5. Scrape the soap mass into heat-resistant molds. Pack well and smooth the top. Cover with plastic wrap and let sit until the soap is cooled. Turn the soap out of the mold. Cut into bars if you haven't used a bar mold. Let air-dry for a week or more, turning the bars so that they dry evenly.

BASIC HAND-MILLING RECIPE, SLOW COOKER METHOD

Keep checking your soap every half hour or so while the soap mass is heating. Depending on the slow cooker and the type of soap you are using, this method can take anywhere from an hour to overnight. You have to experiment to find out what's going to happen.

1 pound shredded plain cold- or hot-process soap, or 1 pound premade soap shreds

4 ounces water
3–6 drops food coloring
1 teaspoon dried herbs

1 teaspoon fragrance oil or essential oil

1. Place the shreds, water, and food coloring in a slow cooker. Cover. Turn the slow cooker to its lowest setting. Let the soap mass heat in the pot for about 15 minutes, or until the pot is up to temperature. Stir gently. (Avoid vigorous stirring to keep the foam level to a minimum.) Let it cook for 30 minutes.

2. Check the soap mass. It may have started to soften, and even become translucent by now. If it hasn't, just be patient; it will. Stir gently.

3. When the soap has taken on a translucent look and you can stir the water all the way through, you are ready to make the additions. Sprinkle the herbs over the mass and stir until evenly distributed.

4. Remove ⅓ cup of the soap mass and place in a glass bowl. Stir the fragrance material into this and then return it to the pan and stir it in thoroughly. If you want to alter the amounts of additives, make further additions and stir well.

5. Scrape the soap mass into heat-resistant molds. Pack well and smooth the top. Cover with plastic wrap and let sit until the soap is cooled. Turn the soap out of the mold. Cut into bars if you haven't used a bar mold. Let air-dry for a week or more, turning the bars so that they'll dry evenly.

BASIC HAND-MILLING RECIPE, MICROWAVE METHOD

Check your soap every 3 minutes while it's heating. Depending on the microwave and the type of soap you're using, this could take 15–30 minutes or more. You must experiment to know exactly what will happen.

1 pound shredded plain cold- or hot-process soap, or

1 pound premade soap shreds

4 ounces water

3–6 drops food coloring

1 teaspoon dried herbs

1 teaspoon fragrance oil or essential oil

1. Place the shreds in a microwave-safe glass bowl. Add the water and food coloring. Stir gently. (Avoid vigorous stirring to keep the foam level to a minimum.)

2. Cover with plastic wrap and place in the microwave oven. Set the oven on medium temperature and set the cooking time to 3 minutes.

3. Using oven mitts, remove the bowl from the microwave. Check the soap mass. It should have started to soften, and even become translucent by now. If it hasn't, just be patient; it will. Stir gently. Continue to heat the soap mass in intervals of 3 minutes, removing each time to check on the status. Be *very careful*; the soap mass will be very hot!

4. When the soap has taken on a translucent look and you can stir the water all the way through, you are ready to make the additions. Be very careful of escaping steam; don't stick your head over the bowl as you stir. Sprinkle the herbs over the mass and stir until evenly distributed. Remove ⅓ cup of the soap mass and place in a glass bowl. Stir the fragrance material into this and then return it to the pan and stir it in thoroughly. If you want to alter the amounts of additives, make further additions and stir well.

5. Scrape the soap mass into heat-resistant molds. Pack well and smooth the top. Be careful about your molds; you can distort or completely melt a mold with the microwave-heated soap mass. Cover with plastic wrap and let sit until the soap is cooled. Turn the soap out of the mold. Cut into bars if you haven't used a bar bold. Let air-dry for a week or more, turning the bars so that they'll dry evenly.

Unmolding

Getting hand-milled soap out of the mold can be a challenge. You'll have to use trial and error. Some batches are just stickier than others. Some may release with no trouble at all, and others may take extended time in the molds before they'll release.

ADDITIVE IDEAS

Using the basic hand-milling recipe, your choice of method, and the additions of extra-rich ingredients in the following recipes make these soaps a luxury. Packed with moisture and precious scent, they're sure to please. Don't save them for too long. Fresh ingredients are best when used within three months.

CHOCOLATE INDULGENCE

1 pound shredded soap
6 ounces milk
1 ounce crushed cocoa butter
1 ounce bittersweet chocolate chips

ROSE FANTASY

1 pound shredded soap
6 ounces rosewater
8–10 drops rose otto
1 teaspoon glycerin

SHEA BUTTER DREAM

1 pound shredded soap
6 ounces orange flower water
1 teaspoon shea butter

RESCUING SOAP BATCHES

Beginning soapers will be happy to hear there are quite a few ways to make use of a less-than-perfect batch of soap.

Rebatching

If you have an ugly, seized batch of cold-process soap or a grainy and spongy batch of hot-process, you can use the hand-milling techniques to transform it into usable soap. This is called rebatching. Don't rebatch soap that is lye-heavy, or has pockets of liquid lye, or lye crystals. Dispose of those kinds of failures in a safe manner. If your "failed" batch is simply ugly or has a strange texture, you can grate it, melt it, and remake it into something useful.

Here's how: Grate the soap as directed for hand milling. Decide what color, scent, and texture materials you want to use. Depending on what is "off" about the batch, you can try to bring the batch to the color or scent you intended, or you could go off on a whole new tangent.

Making Laundry Soap

Another great use for less-than-ideal soap is laundry soap. This is ideal for soap shreds as long as they don't have too high a superfat content, which will get the clothes oily and funky-smelling. Keep the shreds in a plastic pail and cover them with water. The soap will get gelatinous in a couple of days. It will probably be a funny gray color if you've combined a number of scraps from different colored batches.

Scoop about ¼ cup of this gel into the washer and add the water before the clothes. You can use this to boost your regular detergent, and you'll use less. A good rinse for clothes washed with this is made from plain white vinegar infused with citrus peel.

For a fragrant and reusable dryer sheet, make your own! Cut a white cotton terry hand towel into six equally sized pieces. Keep them by the dryer. Put about 10 drops of essential oil on a piece of the fabric when you want to use one. Simply toss into the dryer as you would a disposable sheet.

TEST FIRST

First, test your "failed" batch for mildness. Use litmus paper or phenolphthalein. If the soap is within the neutral range, it's safe to rebatch. If it isn't, prepare it for proper disposal at your local hazardous materials pickup.

CITRUS-VINEGAR LAUNDRY RINSE

1. Fill a large glass jar with citrus peel.
2. Cover the peel with white vinegar and let it sit for at least 3 days.
3. Replace the peels after a few weeks, refilling with vinegar as needed.
4. Use ¼ –½ cup per laundry load.

Another way to make laundry soap is to let the soap shreds dry completely and grind them into powder with a mortar and pestle, or in a food processor. They'll be brittle when they're ready. You can try your blender, but it may not work as well as the other ways. Store the soap powder in an airtight container and use ¼ cup or less per load. Experiment with how much you prefer. You can, of course, make laundry soap from start to finish, on purpose.

LAUNDRY SOAP

Since you won't be using this soap on your hands, you can use an all-coconut, completely saponified recipe. You can add essential or fragrance oil, if you like. You can even buy fragrance oil that smells like a famous detergent.

1 pound soap
8 ounces water
12 ounces lye
4 pounds coconut oil
1–3 tablespoons essential oil or fragrance oil
(optional)

1. Make the batch as usual.
2. Cut the block into small pieces and spread them out on a drying rack.
3. When those pieces are dry and firm, run them through the grater blade on your food processor.
4. Spread the shreds out to dry. When they are very brittle, whirl them ½ cup at a time in the bowl of the food processor, using the regular blade, to make a powder. (Don't process them too long or they'll compact back into a solid mass.)
5. Store the soap powder in an airtight container.

CHAPTER FOURTEEN

MAKE YOUR OWN RECIPES

Now that you have made many batches of soap using various techniques, you're ready to start formulating your own special recipe! It can seem daunting, but when it comes down to it, it's just basic math. Feeling rusty? Many a soapmaker has revisited seventh grade in order to create unique and personal soap formulas.

YOUR INNER CHEMIST

By now, if you've been doing the soap projects in order, you're already familiar with the basics of making soap with lye—fatty acids and caustics. You know that vinegar will neutralize a base (in this case, lye solutions and raw soap). You know that by the time the soap has completely saponified, the fatty acids and caustics have been transformed into soap and glycerin.

WHAT WILL AN OIL DO?

There are some very clear ways of predicting what an oil will do. You look at the chemical makeup of each oil and remember that, with some exceptions, oils that have similar ratios of chemical constituents will behave in similar ways. Combine the "paper" qualities of the oils with your hands-on experience for the best results you can imagine.

Now, it's just a matter of research and a little number crunching, and you can make your ideal soap recipe. As you did at the beginning, start with small batches. Keep track of your experiments, progress, and results.

Refer to your single-oil batches and the batches you've made with different recipes. You may find the extremely clean feeling of coconut oil soap pleasing, whereas lots of people find it drying. Or perhaps you love the rich creaminess of cocoa and shea butters mixed with just a little coconut oil.

ANIMAL OR VEGETABLE?

Deciding whether to use animal or vegetable oils, or a combination of both, is each soapmaker's choice. Excellent soap can be made from either. Most soapmakers use both at some point. No matter which fats and oils you choose to use, research their properties, benefits, and uses in soapmaking. Finding an oil blend that suits you to perfection is one of the most gratifying experiences in soapmaking.

Animal Fats

Common animal fats come from cattle and pigs, but some exotic animal fats, such as emu oil, are gaining great popularity. You can purchase animal fats clean and ready to use, or you can render the fats from meat yourself.

All animal fats, with the exception of butterfat and lanolin, come from slaughtered animals, and are a way of using the entire animal. Hunters often find themselves with fat from deer, elk, and other game that can be rendered into useful soapmaking fat. People who raise small flocks of food animals generally like to put as much of the processed animals to use as possible, and rendering their fat and making it into soap can become another way to accomplish this.

EMU OIL

Emu oil is a by-product of processing the large, flightless birds for meat. The oil is becoming extremely popular in soapmaking and other cosmetic applications. It is reported to have many therapeutic and healing properties. Emu ranching is becoming popular in the United States because emus provide low-fat, high-protein meat.

Lard is the animal fat most accessible to home soapers. You can buy blocks of clean lard, ready for soapmaking, at the grocery store in the section with butter. Lard makes a very hard bar of soap and is favored by many soapmakers.

Butter, of course, comes from milk. Butter may be used as a soapmaking fat, but it has a high rate of rancidity so is best used in small amounts, if at all. Milk soaps use the butterfat from goat and cow milk to great skin-care advantage.

Lanolin is the fat from the wool of sheep, and it is processed out of the fleece after shearing. You are familiar with the scent of lanolin if you've worn a hand-knitted wool sweater. It is very emollient and is best used as a superfatting agent.

Tallow is rendered beef or mutton fat. It's used extensively in shortening and sometimes as a frying agent. At one time it was a main ingredient of candles.

Vegetable Fats

Contemporary soapmaking techniques have made the use of vegetable fats a viable alternative to animal fats. Combining various vegetable oils in specific combinations can produce hard, long-lasting bars. Vegetable oils are readily available, and many are very inexpensive.

NO MINERAL OIL OR PETROLEUM JELLY

Keep in mind that you should never use mineral oil or petroleum jelly in handmade soap, as they do not react with caustics in a way that creates soap. They can be used in small amounts as a superfatting agent, but in general they do not perform well with the water necessary to make soap foam.

There are many reasons some soapers prefer all-vegetable soaps. Vegetable fats tend to be less pore-clogging than animal fat. Some people find the smell of animal fats off-putting, although in a carefully formulated recipe there will be no unpleasant odor. Still others choose to use vegetable fats exclusively because they don't care for the idea of killing animals for human consumption or cosmetic use.

OIL FORMS

You can start with your oils in one of two forms: liquid or solid. Here's the low-down on each.

Liquid Oils

Some oils—such as avocado oil and olive oil—are sold as liquids. To be used in soap, oils must be in a liquid state when mixed with the caustic solution. Liquid oils are, of course, ready to go, and they usually require little if any heating to get them ready to mix. Pouring room-temperature liquid oils into the warmed and melted solid oils is an effective way of helping to lower their temperature to the point necessary for combining the oils with the caustics. Here is a selection of the liquid oils available:

- **Almond oil:** lubricating, occlusive, rich, and moisturizing. It has a short shelf life, so use sparingly.

- **Avocado oil:** a thick, rich oil. High in vitamins, goes rancid slowly, and is very lubricating.

- **Canola oil:** comes from grapeseed oil. Almost completely unsaturated. Can be used similarly to olive oil. Absorbs well on the skin. Needs to be blended with some saturated oils in order to saponify well.

- **Castor oil:** an indispensable oil for soapmakers. It has a specialized chemical makeup that provides an outstanding lather boost to lye soaps. It also helps to bind fragrance. It is a great default superfatting agent. Great in shampoos and transparent soap.

- **Emu oil:** very beneficial in many ways. Good for superfatting. Found to be an extremely healing oil.

- **Grapeseed oil:** is a light, slightly astringent oil. An extremely light oil that lubricates well, but leaves little residue on the skin. It is very light green and has no taste and very little odor. Slightly astringent.

- **Jojoba oil:** actually a liquid wax that comes from the beans of the jojoba tree, native to the southwestern United States. Virtually never goes bad and is similar to the oil in human skin. It is humectant and contributes shelf life and silky feel to soap. Costly. Can be used as part of a formula for a luxury soap, or as a superfatting agent in a basic recipe.

- **Macadamia nut oil:** light, rich, and adds lubrication and silkiness to soap formulas. It has a long shelf life. Like jojoba oil, it is costly so can be reserved for superfatting or can be part of a blend of expensive oils for a luxurious soap.

- **Soybean oil:** light and readily available. Most salad oils sold as "vegetable oil" are made from soy. It absorbs readily, does not clog pores, and is inexpensive. It is best used in combination with richer oils, as on its own it tends to have a weak, unstable lather.

- **Olive oil:** Last but not least is good old olive oil. It is an excellent moisturizer and is the most useful soapmaking oil, overall. True Castile soap is made of 100 percent olive oil from the Castile region of Spain. In soapmaking, lower-grade, less-expensive olive pomace oil makes a hard bar and creates a quicker trace than higher grades. Higher grades of olive oil—such as virgin and extra-virgin—make hard soap with a lower foam, although the soap dissolves very easily when left exposed to water. Olive oils range from light gold to deep green and can affect the color of the finished soap.

Solid Oils

Other oils—such as coconut oil and lard—are sold as solids. Solid oils must be melted before they can be mixed with the caustic solutions. Melting points vary from just above room temperature to quite a bit higher, so you'll need to be sure to plan carefully to avoid getting the oil solution too hot. Never let oils come to a boil and never leave heating oils unattended. A good way to melt solid oils is to place them in heated liquid oils and let them liquefy as they bring down the temperature of the overall solution. Here is a selection of the solid oils available:

- **Coconut oil:** creates the billowy, stable lather prized in handmade soap. It should be used in combination with emollient oils to counteract coconut's potential to create a drying soap.

- **Solid vegetable shortening:** made from mostly soy oil, sometimes with cottonseed oil added, depending on brand and season. You can make a serviceable and inexpensive soap from just this oil.

- **Lard:** fat that comes from the areas around the kidneys of pigs. Makes a very hard bar on its own, but without other oils it has a low, slippery lather. Best used in combination with vegetable oils that have properties it lacks.

- **Mango butter:** yellow and grainy. An excellent superfatting agent and adds rich silkiness to soaps. It has a long shelf life.

- **Palm oil:** one of the primary soapmaking oils. It contributes hardness and body to soap formulas. You can use it at between 20 percent and 30 percent in soap formulas.

- **Palm kernel oil:** can be used in combination with coconut and olive to create a hard, long-lasting bar with lots of glycerin. It releases a large amount of glycerin.

- **Shea butter:** made from the seeds of the karite tree of West Africa. Use in quantity for a very luxurious soap. It works well as a superfatting agent.

- **Tallow:** used to make soap for centuries. Tallow comes from cows and game animals such as deer, moose, and elk. You can render tallow on your own or buy it from a renderer. It is more difficult to find than lard.

EXOTIC OILS

With so many people making soap, many formerly "exotic" oils such as emu and mango butter have become relatively commonplace. There are still, however, many oils that, for various reasons, remain exotic. One of the factors in making this list is price. Another is how new the oil is on the soapmaking scene. Yet another factor is limited-use oils, for example those that have an unpleasant smell but are very useful for specific application. Here is a selection of the exotic oils available:

- **Babassu oil:** a rich, penetrating oil that does not clog pores. Use as a superfatting agent or as part of a luxury formula.

- **Evening primrose oil:** quite costly, but reputedly excellent for dry skin, eczema, and psoriasis. Supposedly has other healing properties including relieving the symptoms of fibromyalgia, chronic fatigue syndrome, and arthritis.

- **Hemp seed oil:** has a reputation as a soothing, healing oil, particularly for dry skin. It contains none of the drug THC, so it hasn't any dangerous properties. Use as a superfatting agent due to the fact that it is prone to rancidity and in large amounts may contribute to spoilage.

- **Kokum butter:** very moisturizing, yet good for dehydrated, acne-prone skin because it is lubricating without clogging pores. It contributes hardness in a soap formula as well as non-greasy moisturizing.

- **Kukui nut oil:** from Hawaii, an excellent skin conditioner and reported to have many healing properties. It lubricates without oiliness. Use as a superfatting agent or as part of a luxury soap.

- **Neem oil:** said to possess healing properties of such great proportion that soapmakers are willing to overlook the fact that it smells horrible. Use as a base oil for problem skin or as part of a formula for a "healing" bar.

- **Sal butter:** has a long shelf life and makes an excellent superfatting agent. It is lubricating but not greasy.

As you make more and more soap, you may find that one or more of these "exotics" becomes commonplace in your soapmaking. If you find an oil not listed here, go ahead and experiment with it and share your results. Eventually someone will want to know what you have learned!

FATTY ACIDS

The fatty acid profile of an oil or fat determines the way it behaves in a soap formula. Fatty acids are the individual components that make up the oil or fat. A fatty acid is comprised of a carboxylic acid group and a hydrocarbon chain. Saturated fatty acids are solid at room temperature; unsaturated fatty acids are fluid at room temperature. Studying the fatty acid components of soapmaking oils can help you determine which oils to use for the effect you want. These are the most important fatty acids for soapmaking:

- **Lauric:** extremely effective cleanser; can be harsh; good lather

- **Linoleic:** goes rancid easily; use in small amounts in combination with more stable oils; contributes mildness; conditioning; polyunsaturated (likely to oxidize)

- **Linolenic:** double bonds; prone to rancidity; not that prevalent in soapmaking oils

- **Myristic:** softest of the saturates; can be harsh; hard bar; good lather

- **Oleic:** long shelf life; conditioning; main component of olive oil; monounsaturated

- **Palmitic:** saturated; long shelf life; hard bar; stable lather

- **Palmitoleic:** long shelf life

- **Ricinoleic:** castor oil; has an alcohol component; conditioning; monounsaturated

- **Stearic:** saturated; hard bar; stable lather

Here are the primary fatty acids in some common soapmaking oils:

- **Almond oil:** mostly oleic

- **Apricot oil:** mostly oleic, .25 linoleic

- **Avocado oil:** mostly oleic

- **Castor oil:** mostly linoleic

- **Cocoa butter:** .33 oleic, .3 palmitic, .33 stearic

- **Coconut oil:** mostly lauric

- **Emu oil:** .45 to .50 oleic, .22 to .25 palmitic, .08 to .10 stearic, .06 to .10 linoleic

- **Grapeseed oil:** linoleic

- **Hemp seed oil:** mostly linoleic

- **Kokum butter:** .67 stearic, .28 oleic, .03 palmitic

- **Kukui nut oil:** .48 linoleic

- **Lard:** .41 oleic, .22 palmitic, .15 stearic, .12 linoleic

- **Macadamia nut oil:** mostly oleic

- **Mango butter:** .33 to .5 linoleic, .25 to .5 stearic

- **Olive oil:** mostly oleic

- **Palm oil:** about .5 palmitic, over .3 oleic

- **Palm kernel oil:** about .5 lauric

- **Sal butter:** .47 stearic, .44 oleic, .04 palmitic

- **Shea butter:** .5 oleic, .3 to .5 stearic

- **Soybean oil:** mostly linoleic

- **Tallow:** .36 oleic, .25 palmitic, .9 lauric, .19 stearic, .03 myristic

Some oils are excellent superfatters:

- **Castor oil:** Used for shampoos, transparent soaps, and for superfatting cold- and hot-process opaque soap; the best superfatting agent for boosting lather

- **Kokum butter:** Great for superfatting; similar to shea butter

- **Mango butter:** Use in small amounts for superfatting

- **Sal butter:** Doesn't get rancid, adds emollient quality

- **Shea butter:** Makes a very luxe, hard bar; also great for superfatting

SAPONIFICATION VALUES (SAP VALUES)

The saponification value of an oil indicates how much lye it takes to turn 1 ounce of that oil into soap. The saponification values for sodium hydroxide and potassium hydroxide lyes are different. If you use both types of caustics, be extra certain of what you're working with when you make your calculations.

TABLE OF SAPONIFICATION VALUES						
Oil	Sodium Hydroxide	Potassium Hydroxide		Oil	Sodium Hydroxide	Potassium Hydroxide
Almond oil	.136	.1904		Kokum butter	.140	.19
Apricot oil	.135	.189		Kukui nut oil	.135	.189
Avocado oil	.133	.1862		Lanolin	.074	.1037
Babassu oil	.175	.2450		Lard	.138	.1932
Beef tallow	.140	.1967		Macadamia nut oil	.139	.1946
Beeswax	.069	.0966		Mango butter	.140	.190
Canola oil	.124	.1736		Moose tallow	.139	.193
Castor oil	.128	.18		Neem oil	.138	.1941
Cocoa butter	.137	.1918		Olive oil	.134	.1876
Coconut oil	.190	.2660		Palm kernel oil	.156	.2184
Deer tallow	.138	.193		Palm oil	.141	.1974
Duck fat	.137	.1916		Sal butter	.135	.190
Emu oil	.135	.195		Shea butter	.128	.1792
Evening primrose oil	.136	.190		Sheep tallow	.138	.1936
Grapeseed oil	.126	.177		Solid vegetable shortening	.136	.1904
Hemp seed oil	.136	.188		Soy oil	.135	.189
Jojoba oil	.069	.0966				

Note that some of the more exotic fats and oils that have been added relatively recently to the soapmaking roster may vary widely in actual SAP value. If you're using shea butter, mango butter, sal butter, or grapeseed oil, be certain to check with your supplier for exact SAP value.

MAKING WORKSHEETS

No matter how proficient you are at computer spreadsheets, make your first worksheets with good old-fashioned paper, pencil, and a calculator. Many soapers get off track by spending valuable soaping time setting up the spreadsheet. Once you've mastered the paper-and-pencil method, set it up on a computer spreadsheet, if you like.

Even if you decide to use lye calculations or a spreadsheet you've created, make sure you know what you're doing without one. It's not that the calculator will let you down, it's just good practice to be able to rely on your own skills. When you make your first formulas, a lye calculator is a great way to check your work.

A pad of graph paper is a useful tool. A pencil with a good eraser is another good one. You don't need a fancy calculator, just one you can use with ease.

First Calculation

Multiply the SAP value of a particular oil by the number of ounces of that oil. The resulting number indicates the amount of lye in ounces that is needed to achieve saponification.

For recipes that use a number of different oils, you calculate how much lye you need for each oil and add the lye amounts to get the 100 percent SAP rate. If you make soap with the exact SAP value, you will have no leftover oil in the batch. Because this leaves you no margin for error, there is a possibility that using the exact 100 percent SAP value could create a lye-heavy batch. It is smart soapmaking practice to use a "lye discount" to ensure a gentle soap.

Taking a Lye Discount

Here is an example of how to take a lye discount; that is, how to alter your lye ratios to make sure you have oils left in your soap after the saponification process.

Coconut oil has a SAP value of .19 when using sodium hydroxide. A recipe that uses 10 ounces of coconut oil would require $10 \times .19$ ounces of lye, or 1.9 ounces to saponify it 100 percent.

A lye discount is a reduction from the total amount of lye needed to saponify the oils to a lesser amount, ensuring there is some oil left over in the soap. It's always a good idea to plan for some extra oil to ensure mildness. Too much extra oil, however, can lead to soft soap that spoils easily. A good discount to aim for is between 5 and 8 percent.

For a 10 percent lye reduction in the coconut oil example, multiply 1.9 (the amount of lye) by .1 (10 percent). You get .19 ounces. So, to take a 10 percent discount, you subtract .19 from 1.9 to get 1.71 ounces of lye. To take a smaller lye discount, follow the same formula using smaller multiples: .02, .03, .04, .05, and so on.

Here's a look at a hypothetical all-coconut batch in three sizes.

LYE SAPONIFICATION DISCOUNT TABLE			
	1-pound batch	**4-pound batch**	**8-pound batch**
Coconut oil	.190 × 16 =	.190 × 64=	.190 × 128 =
Water	6 ounces	24 ounces	48 ounces
Lye (100% saponification)	3.04 ounces	12.16 ounces	24.32 ounces
Lye discount 1%	.0304	.1216	.2432
Lye discount 2%	.0608	.2432	.4864
Lye discount 3%	.0912	.3648	.7296
Lye discount 4%	.1216	.4864	.9728
Lye discount 5%	.152	.608	1.216
Lye discount 6%	.1824	.7296	1.4592
Lye discount 7%	.2128	.8512	1.7024
Lye discount 8%	.2432	.9728	1.9456
Lye discount 9%	.2736	1.0944	2.1888
Lye discount 10%	.304	1.216	2.432

You are seeing lots and lots of decimal places. Always round down for lye because it is always better to have a little less than you need than a little more.

More Excess Oils: Superfatting

You can add oils after the initial saponification in the soap pan to superfat your soap. Taking a lye discount is actually a way of superfatting, but it reduces the amount of base oils from the outset. When you superfat, you add the oils when the soap is traced, and in theory this is kinder to the oils.

Because you're adding the oils when the soap is traced, you can superfat with more expensive luxury oils and keep their properties, whereas if you added them at the beginning, they'd become more of the discounted base subjected to the most active lye, thereby losing some of the nutrient value. Whether this is actually what happens is up for debate, but it seems to make sense, so many soapmakers follow this pattern.

> **SHORTCUT**
>
> *A simplified version of this method involves adding 1 tablespoon of superfatting agent per 1 pound of fats. You should do this with a soap formula that already has about 6 percent lye discount, just to be sure. Not every superfatting oil has the same SAP value, of course, but this puts you in a safe range and saves you some math.*

You can calculate the combined total lye discount when you create your formula. For example, if you want a total lye discount of 8 percent, you can take a 4 percent lye discount right off the top, and add enough superfatting oils at trace to create another 4 percent discount, bringing the total up to 8 percent.

Going back to our SAP chart, note that a 4 percent lye discount on a 1-pound batch is .1216 ounces. Thus, for 16 ounces of coconut oil, use 2.9 ounces of lye (3.04 – .1216) to achieve a 4 percent discount. To increase the lye discount to 8 percent, superfat with an additional 4 percent oils at trace. So for 16 ounces of oil, add .64 ounces (16 × .04) of superfatting agent.

Sample Oils Batch

Here's an exercise in calculating a soap formula. You can use the formula hypothetically, or you can actually make soap with it. This is an example using what many beginning soapmakers find that they have on hand. Once you've done this math on this one, go ahead and recalculate it for what you actually have.

Let's say you have accumulated small samples of exotic oils and you want to make soap with them, for a mixed luxury batch. You have 2-ounce samples of almond oil, avocado oil, jojoba oil, macadamia nut oil, mango butter, and shea butter. You also have on hand your usual olive oil, palm oil, palm kernel oil, coconut oil, and castor oil.

Using the "keep the coconut to a third of the formula" rule, see what you can come up with. You have 12 ounces of fancy oils. For those 12 ounces to equal $2/3$ of your total, you will need 6 ounces of coconut oil. That comes to a total of 18 ounces of oils. So this is a "little over 1 pound" batch.

You're going to superfat with castor oil to boost lather, and since you usually use 1 tablespoon of castor per pound of fats, you will use a little more than 1 tablespoon. Use 6 ounces of water. Now, you need to calculate the lye. You'll multiply the SAP value of each special oil by two and the coconut by six (to reflect the number of ounces of each). Then, you'll add up all the lye for the complete SAP value of the recipe:

- **Almond oil:** 2 × .136 = .272

- **Avocado oil:** 2 × .133 = .266

- **Coconut oil:** 6 × .19 = 1.14

- **Jojoba oil:** 2 × .069 = .138

- **Macadamia nut oil:** 2 × .139 = .278

- **Mango butter:** 2 × .14 = .28

- **Shea butter:** 2 × .128 = .256

Raw lye calculation = 2.63, rounded to 2.61.6 ounces.

Then, take your lye discount. For this recipe, make it 4 percent, with another 1 percent or so from the tablespoon of castor oil for superfat:

- 2.6 × 0.04 = 0.1052064 ounce discount

- 2.6 – .064 = 1.536, rounded to 1.5 ounces lye

So! Do you feel like a soapmaker? If you've gone this far, it's a good bet you are. If you aren't yet, get busy! Make some soap already!

CHAPTER FIFTEEN

PRESENTING AND GIFTING YOUR SOAP

Gracious and generous presentations of handmade soap make beautiful gifts. The variety of color, texture, shape, and fragrance in your handmade soaps provides the opportunity to create gift packs and baskets to delight the senses. No matter what the occasion, gifts of handmade soap are sure to be a hit.

REASONS TO GIVE YOUR SOAP AWAY

It isn't completely clear exactly when the soapmaker will find his or her new hobby getting completely out of hand. Perhaps it's when every horizontal service area in your home is covered with curing soap. It could be when you go to prepare the guest room for a dear friend and find nowhere for her to sleep, let alone put down her suitcase. Instead of "When's dinner?" perhaps you're hearing your family ask "Is that soap or food?" Whatever the signal is, eventually it becomes clear that you must start giving your soap away. It can be difficult to be willing to find new homes for your creations. You've planned your soap, created it, tended it, and you may have become very attached to it. However, there are many reasons to give your soap away.

Releasing Your Creativity

Creativity can get bogged down when an artist holds on to too many past projects. Learning to let go can be extremely stimulating. Keeping favorites for reference isn't the same as keeping an untouchable stock of projects. When an artist clears out old projects, the resulting sense of freedom can be quite inspiring.

Donating to Charity

Charity is good for everyone. Your soap is a useful donation to make to shelters. Many soapers regularly donate less-than-perfect but still perfectly useful creations to women and children's shelters, for example. Not everyone realizes that along with food, toiletries including soap are greatly needed. Find a shelter in your area and make a donation of your wonderful handmade soap.

A good way to make soap for donation is to save up soap scraps in semi-disposable food storage containers. When the container is nearly full of scraps, make plain soap to pour over it to fill the mold. You can let this chunked soap cure in the containers and deliver it to the donation location. Put instructions on how to unmold and cut the soap into bars. It is easy to transport and store if you package it this way.

Giving a Gift

Giving gifts of your handmade soap to family and friends is satisfying for all involved. Whether you create a gift suite from start to finish, or you just grab a prettily wrapped bar on your way out to a party, a gift of soap will be appreciated. Appreciated at first, these gifts of soap will very likely become requested, even not-so-gently demanded. The avid crafter can combine crafts to create exquisite gifts. The beginning crafter can be inspired to create elegant, simple presentations.

MAKING SIMPLE GIFTS

There are several easy ways to transform your soaps from simple bars to lovely packages. Here are a few ideas, but really, the sky's the limit.

Cigar Band Wrapper

A simple "cigar band" wrapper is an elegant and easy way to wrap a bar of soap. The name of this style of wrap comes from the practice of placing a small ring of paper around a cigar to indicate the type and maker. You create a band of paper on a larger scale to fit around your bar of soap.

To decide the size to cut the paper, measure around the bar with a tape measure or wrap a piece of paper or string around the bar and measure that. You will have an easier time fastening the ends of the paper if they overlap by about ½". Sometimes you will want to cover the bar end-to-end with a wide band, and other times you'll want a narrower band that doesn't conceal the soap.

The easiest way to fix the ends once you've wrapped the soap is with a small piece of clear tape. For a more finished look, used double-sided tape. Place the small piece of tape under one end of the band and press it down firmly to fix it to the other side. You can also use a glue stick to fasten the bands. Wrap the paper around the bar, and apply a small amount of glue to the inside of the overlapping edge. Press the glued side to the other side and press firmly.

Wrapping Paper

Plain paper and pretty ribbon is a good combination. Simple cord and extravagant paper is another. Choose a "signature" paper in which you present all your soap, or choose a style of paper that you vary in color to coordinate with the soap.

You can find beautiful mulberry and composed handmade papers at art supply stores. A large sheet of paper will make a large number of bands, so although the paper may be expensive, one sheet will go a long way.

WRAPPING PAPER

Regular wrapping paper available at the drugstore can be perfect. Colored tissue is extremely useful. Try distressing it for a casual look, or press with an iron on low temperature before wrapping, for a more tailored look.

Try bands of varying widths until you find the one that looks good to you for each paper and soap. Try cutting with straight scissors as well as with decorative-edge scissors. Sometimes a fancy edge is perfect, but sometimes it's better saved for another use.

Your fabric store will have myriad options for ties. Yarn, cord, ribbon, rick-rack, and even seam binding can be used to great effect. Look for specialty millinery supply houses for fancy, vintage, and unique ribbons. Raffia, which is available in many colors, is perfect for tying soap.

Felted Soap

Felting is a way of treating wool fleece or yarn in such a way that it shrinks and gets fuzzy. Knitters everywhere knit huge purses, throw them into very hot water in the washer, and then agitate them for an extended time, like what we used to call ruining a sweater. The result is a soft, woolly, normal-sized purse. Felted soap is not only decorative, it is also functional as a gentle, simple way to have an "all in one" washcloth and soap. The wool is gentler than loofah or plastic mesh "scrubbies."

In this case, the wool is in "pre-yarn" form, and rather than an over-sized knitted pouch for the soap—which you could do as well—you wrap thin sheets of carded wool around the soap, then shrink them into place by rubbing the wool-covered soap under hot water. The wool shrinks, and as you rub it in your hands and over an abrasive surface, it makes a tough fabric that continues to shrink as it is used.

FELTED SOAP

A hard, high-foaming soap works best for this project.

Wool roving or cleaned and combed fleece pulled into 3 flat sheets (Use sheets big enough to overlap around the back of the soap just a little.)

Fully cured and dried soap bar or sphere

Washboard, wire mesh, or other sturdy abrasive surface that won't be damaged by hot water

1. Wrap the wool or fleece sheets around the soap, one at a time, alternating directions.

2. Take the wool-covered soap to the kitchen sink and turn on the faucet, making the water as hot as your hands can stand for an extended time.

3. Turn the faucet down to a thin stream. Hold the wool-covered soap in the stream, turning it so that it's all wet, but do not use so much water that the wool slips off.

4. Turn off the water and begin to squeeze and rub the woolly soap, smoothing any ends of the wool that try to come loose. (It should start matting pretty quickly.) To enhance the matting, rub the shrinking wool on the rough side of the washboard or wire mesh.

5. Turn the water back on and work the wool-covered soap into a lather, squeezing and rinsing. It will have shrunk considerably and should have completely covered the soap on all sides.

6. When the felt is firm and there are no gaps, turn off the water and squeeze the felted soap in a towel to remove excess water. Place it out of the sun in a well-ventilated area to dry. Or if you are going to use it right away, just head for the shower!

Small Boxes

Small boxes can be decorated to hold one or more bars of soap. Little boxes can be found in office supply, jewelry supply, and packaging supply stores. Small folded take-out boxes, such as those often used by Chinese restaurants, are very cute containers for bars of soap. Place a couple of prettily wrapped bars in the container and make a label for the container out of the same paper you used to wrap the soap.

Computer-Generated Labels and Tags

Whether your computer skills are basic or advanced, you can use your computer as a tool for creating professional-looking labels and tags for your soap. Even the most basic word-processing program can produce tidy printing in varying sizes.

To get ideas about how to create the layouts for your labels, refer to labels on food and cosmetic jars. For example, you can use a large font size for the name of the soap, which you want to be the main thing people see, and a smaller font size for the ingredients and notes for use. If you really want to get fancy, list a couple of things that make the soap special and list the ingredients in order of how much of each is in the soap, greatest to least.

Plastic Wrap and Bags

You can use stretchy cling-film to wrap melt-and-pour soaps to protect them. Cut a square of wrap a few inches bigger than the bar. Place the bar in the middle, face down. Gather up the edges and gently pull it tight over the surface of the bar. Twist tightly, cut close to the soap, and fix with a piece of tape or a sticker.

NO PLASTIC FOR LYE

Remember that plastic wrap is not the best packaging for lye soaps, since they need to have air circulation to prevent spoilage. If you shrink wrap them, use wrap that has tiny circulation holes, and leave the ends unwrapped.

Stiff plastic bags commonly called "cellophane" bags are an excellent presentation material. You can tie the top with raffia, decorative yarn, or ribbon or you can neatly fold the opening shut and seal it with a pretty sticker.

Another useful plastic wrap is shrink wrap. You can buy shrink wrap in various sizes at craft stores and through the Internet. Shrink wrap is placed around the soap, fixed with tape if necessary, and heated with a special heat tool. There are some shrink wraps that are designed to be used with the high setting on a blow-dryer. Shrink wrap can lend a finished look to your soap if it's done neatly. You can purchase shrink wrap that will let you smell the bar of soap through it. Shop Internet soap supply houses for this and other shrink-wrap products created with the soapmaker in mind.

DESIGNING A GIFT SUITE

A carefully planned gift project can take a good two months or more, so get ready to plan ahead! Soap gift packages can be planned in stages, so you can tailor your project to fit your time. From start to finish, a coordinated presentation is a rewarding project. Be sure to keep records and take photographs for reference.

When you give a gift of handmade soap, be sure to include some information about the soap somewhere in the packaging. Many people have never used handmade soap and are not aware of some of the attributes that make it special. The main thing is to let the person know that the soap shouldn't sit in water between uses. Let them know that the solid lye soaps need air and that the casting soaps need to be kept airtight. Include the expected shelf life as well.

Planning Ahead

In order to be able to have just the right soap on hand to go into your special presentations, you need to do some planning. One way to do this is to keep a calendar with holidays, birthdays, and upcoming events marked on it. If you know that your friend's wedding and Father's Day are both coming up in June, you can plan your crafting and soapmaking time in May to prepare for these projects.

If you're making cold-process soap, you need to make it at least four weeks before the day you plan to put together your gift basket. You may also need this long to shop for supplies and order through the Internet. Hot-process soaps, including liquid and transparent, are best if they're made at least a week ahead. That gives opaque hot process time to dry out a bit and the clear soaps time to settle or become clearer.

Sure, you can make a half dozen bars of beautiful casting soap in an hour. However, you also need time to make labels, wrap and package the soaps, and assemble the basket. It is easy to underestimate the time you'll need to complete a project. This can leave you stressed out and tired, which you definitely want to avoid.

Multitask

You can multitask and make some elements you'll need later while you make the ones for the project at hand. For example, if you're making cold-process soap for a party next month and you want to make a chunked soap for the month after that, make more than you need for the party and cut the rest into chunks to use in the next project. The same thing goes for melt-and-pour and hot-process soap. With just a little planning, you can always get a jump on what's coming next.

> ### QUALITY IN GIFTS
>
> *If your soaps are not neutral, have too much dye, leak excess oil, or have other characteristics of poor soaping, no amount of beautiful packaging can make up for that fact. Make sure your soaps are of high quality before you give them away. They don't have to be beautiful, just safe to use.*

If you're making up a number of the same baskets, set up an assembly line. It's even more fun if you have a few friends to help on a big project. Promises of your soap will get you lots of volunteers.

GIFT COLLECTION IDEAS

Here are some ideas to get you started on ways to present your soaps. Some of the soaps have recipes in the book, and others you get to make up on your own. Use the suggested names and descriptions in the soap listings as prompts for you to create your unique soaps. You have the skills, or, at the very least, the book in hand, to acquire the skills. Don't follow each "go with" suggestion as if it were gospel. Use what you like, adjust to what you have or can get, and forget what doesn't appeal to you.

When crafting, many people spend too much time hunting for exactly what they saw in a book, and not taking into account their own innate creativity. You can learn more from the way you adapt these suggestions than by following them to the letter:

ALL NATURAL

- **Soaps:** Unscented, uncolored bars made with only herbs or grains for texture, plant colorants, and essential oils for fragrance

- **Wrap:** Brown kraft paper

- **Tie:** Plain cotton string or garden twine

- **Label:** Use a pair of decorative-edge scissors to cut paper into a folded hang-tag; write the information about the soap on the tag and hang it from the tie with cotton string

- **Container:** Natural-color wicker basket or folded or crimped brown paper bag

VALENTINE PRESENT

- **Soaps:** Heart-in-Circle casting soap in tube mold, Pink and White Swirl cold process, Vanilla and Chocolate cream soap

- **Wrap:** Red cellophane bags, heart-print fabric, or red or ivory silk dupioni fabric

- **Tie:** Red and white satin ribbons or cord

- **Container:** Heart-shaped candy box or heart-shaped basket

GARDENER'S GIFT

- **Soaps:** Fresh Herb hand milled; Tomato Leaf melt and pour; Basil hot process; Cucumber liquid hand wash; Sage, Rosemary, and Thyme shower gel; and Gardener's Grit Special cream soap

- **Wrap:** Garden-themed wrapping paper or handmade paper with leaves or petals, color coordinated to the soap

- **Tie:** Garden twine
- **Container:** Terra cotta flower pot, trug-shaped basket, small bushel-style basket, or berry basket

THANKSGIVING PRESENTATION

- **Soaps:** Pumpkin Spice cold process, Mulled Cider hot process, Falling Leaves casting soap, Autumn Jewels transparent soap, Fall Festival liquid soap, and Turning Leaves cream soap
- **Wrap:** Warm-toned papers or harvest-theme fabric
- **Tie:** Orange raffia or maroon velvet ribbon
- **Container:** Cornucopia-shaped basket

CHRISTMAS GLOW

- **Soaps:** Holiday Lights transparent, Santa's Special cream shaving soap, Embedded Star in Circle slices
- **Wrap:** Clear or colored transparent cellophane bags and gold and silver tissue paper
- **Tie:** Gold and silver stretch cording
- **Container:** Cut glass bowl

HANUKKAH GIFTS

- **Soaps:** Carrot Spice hand milled, Blue and silver casting soap made in dreidel-shaped chocolate molds, Casting soap loaf with eight-candle design, Casting soap "latkes," Bitter herb cream soap
- **Wrap:** Pretty blue handmade paper or iridescent white paper
- **Tie:** Silver and blue metallic ribbon
- **Container:** Silver metal basket with white cloth

DINO BIRTHDAY PARTY

- **Soap:** Dinosaurs in amber melt and pour, Frog and Slime in clear bag, Rough and Tough Scrub-Up cream soap, Black Tar liquid soap
- **Wrap:** Dino print gift bags
- **Tie:** Green plastic string
- **Container:** Metal tool box or burlap sack

ZOO BIRTHDAY PARTY

- **Soap:** Casting soaps embedded with animals such as elephants, zebras, tigers, and snakes, and Zebra- and Tiger-Striped casting soap slices
- **Wrap:** Animal-print fabric or burlap
- **Tie:** Thin rope or raffia
- **Container:** Canvas zoo-keeper's hat

BRIDESMAID'S GIFT

- **Soap:** Casting soap in rose mold in the colors of the wedding, rich and gentle facial soap with rose otto and neroli essential oils, and shimmering shower gel

- **Wrap:** Silk and organdy coordinated with the wedding colors

- **Tie:** Satin ribbons in the wedding colors

- **Container:** A hat box with gold printing

MOTHER'S DAY

- **Soap:** Casting soap to match her bathroom, liquid hand soap for the kitchen, guest soaps to match her guest bathroom, and luxury soap with rose and jasmine essential oils

- **Wrap:** Elegant organza bags

- **Tie:** Satin ribbons to coordinate with the soap

- **Container:** Pretty fabric-covered box to match her dresser that she can use for other things

FATHER'S DAY

- **Soaps:** Cold-process Shaving Soap rounds, Rosemary-Mint liquid soap, Forest Green casting soap slices with tree embed

- **Wrap:** Waxed paper folded neatly like wrapping paper, or glassine bags

- **Tie:** Green twine from gardening section, or brown and green raffia

- **Container:** Attractive box that is useful on his dresser, or a mini tool or tackle box

PACKAGING ELEMENTS

As you head to the back of your local craft store, searching for soap supplies, you may have walked down one of the aisles bursting with design elements intended for scrapbooking and other paper crafts. Or, you may be a dedicated "cropper" with much scrapbooking experience and a stash of beautiful treasures.

All those stickers, rubber stamps, embellishments, and beautiful papers can be pressed into service as exquisite presentation materials for your soapy creations. A small packet of colored paper bags and a sheet of seasonal stickers is a wonderful and easy alternative to presenting your hostess with a bar of soap in the plastic sandwich bag you grabbed on your way out the door to dinner with friends.

Rubber stamps on blocks and the kind of stamps with a band of changeable letters can work well for embossing soap and stamping the label you use to package it. Be sure to clean your stamps of soap residue that may decay the rubber and metals over time. Borrowing from another craft, stepping stone making, you can find sets of individual letters that will make clear imprints on your soap.

Select a set of stickers or other embellishment that suits the nature of your gift. You can go by event theme (such as birthday, graduation, or anniversary), by season, or by the nature of the soap itself (such as a nature-oriented decoration for an all-natural bar or a tropical theme for coconut-scented soaps). Select papers and ribbon to coordinate, add fancy-edge scissors or a shaped paper punch, and all you have to do is put it together.

You'll find a few examples following. Using this approach if you're selling your soap is not going to be economical, but for ease in assembling a single gift or a small number of items, these materials are perfect. Encourage the happy recipient of your gift to actually use the soap, no matter how pretty it is.

STICKERS

Besides using them on the papers you use to wrap bars of soap, you can use stickers on the containers you use for liquid soap, shower gels, and cream soaps. Since they are not intended for use in a wet environment they will probably come off, but you might be pleasantly surprised.

～ SEASHORE ～

Sheer white vellum
Seashell vellum stickers

Wrap chunky bars all the way, like a package. Embellish with shell stickers, letting the stickers fold around the corners.

～ THANKSGIVING ～

Pearlized gold paper
Dimensional Thanksgiving theme stickers

Cut the paper into wide cigar-bands that reach all the way to the edge of the soap. Carefully place a sticker in the center of the large surface.

～ BABY SHOWER ～

Pearlized pink and blue paper
Hanging metal baby shower–themed charm
Pastel raffia

Make cigar-band wrappers from the paper. Thread the charms onto coordinating pastel raffia. Tie to suspend the charm in the center of the front surface.

～ BUTTERFLIES ～

Pearlized pink paper
Dimensional butterfly stickers

Cut wide cigar bands and wrap the bars. Affix stickers to bend around the corners.

SHELF LIFE

Handmade soap is gentle and free of excessive preservatives. That fact, however, is one of the few caveats involved with making soap at home. Handmade soap has a shelf life—a time after which it isn't as fresh as it might be.

Signs that soap has passed its shelf life vary from variety to variety. With lye soaps, an "off" or rancid odor is a sign that your soap has gone bad. If you use a high degree of lye discounting and superfatting, this will happen sooner than if you have a more completely saponified bar.

All soaps, including casting soap, will display signs of age by yellowing and changing texture from firm and smooth to warped, grainy, or slimy. Liquid and cream soaps can grow mold, particularly if not preserved. You can prevent premature spoilage through appropriate storage and careful use of cosmetic-grade preservative. Every soap, though, will pass a point of no return if not used in time.

STORING SOAP

Keep soap at its best through proper storage. Don't store soap in sealed plastic storage boxes or bags. Store soap out of direct sunlight. Keep your soap where it won't be exposed to extreme shifts in humidity and temperature.

Sealing lye soap in plastic will cause rancidity. Soap that gets lots of direct sunlight will heat up and cool down, causing rancidity through breakdown of oils, and scent and color will fade. Soap that is exposed to high humidity can get slimy because the glycerin in the soap is a humectant; it attracts moisture from the air.

Curing

If you make soap on a limited basis—2 or 3 pounds at a time, for example—you can easily use a shelf on a bookcase for curing and storage. If you find yourself continually running out of room, get a set of plastic shelves you can put up and take down as needed. And if you get to the stage where you are a constant soapmaker, you may as well just give in and buy or make a soap-curing/storage rack.

USE BY "SELL BY" DATE

Use soap in the order it was made. Be sure to keep "made on" and "use by" dates on your soap storage boxes and racks.

You can modify a bookcase or start from scratch to create your soap rack. The best ones have surfaces of wire mesh. Heavy wire mesh with ⅓" openings works great. Shelves that slide out for loading are ideal. Place freshly cut soaps on the rack, spaced about ½–1" apart. Turn the soaps every few days to be sure they dry evenly. After a few weeks, when the surfaces are dry to the touch, you can stack them more closely. Try to space your soapmaking so that you can rotate partially cured soap out as you place the freshly cut soaps.

After Curing

After a month of curing, cardboard or paperboard shoeboxes are useful for storing your soap. Line the box with plain paper—brown kraft paper is good. Place the soaps loosely in the box. Cut ventilation holes in the lid and sides so that the soap will be protected from light and dust and still get some air.

Be sure to always label your storage system with soap variety, date created, cure date, move to storage date, expected expiration date, and other information that will help you remember the details about each batch. Observe and record the changes your soap goes through as it ages. Again, keeping records is one of your most useful tools in progressing in your craft.

SOAPMAKING RESOURCES

WEBSITES

TRADE ORGANIZATIONS

Handcrafted Soap & Cosmetics Guild
International nonprofit trade organization
www.soapguild.org

Indie Business Network
Donna Maria Coles Johnson's networking and support organization for makers and suppliers of handmade toiletries
www.indiebusinessnetwork.com

RESOURCE SITES

Botanical.com
A great resource for information on herbs
www.botanical.com

Saponifier Magazine
Online magazine for soapmakers and soapmaking community
http://saponifier.com

TEACHING SITES

Rebecca's Soap Delicatessen
www.soapdelicatessen.com/make-soap.html

Teach Soap
http://teachsoap.com

SUPPLIERS

Bramble Berry
Large selection of soapmaking supplies, including Lab Colors and foaming bath butter
www.brambleberry.com

Camden-Grey Essential Oils
Essential oils and soap supplies
www.camdengrey.com

From Nature With Love
Comprehensive soap supply
www.from-nature-with-love.com

Majestic Mountain Sage
Comprehensive soapmaking supply and the original online lye calculator
www.thesage.com

Milky Way Molds
Catherine Failor's outstanding line of soap molds and stamps
www.milkywaymolds.com

Natural Oils International
Excellent source of base oils
www.naturaloils.com

Rainbow Meadow
Essential oils and fragrance oils and soapmaking supplies
www.rainbowmeadow.com

Soul Gazer Sundries

Templates and spreadsheets for soapers

www.soulgazersundries.com

SunFeather Handmade Bodycare

Sandy Maine's pioneering company

www.sunsoap.com

Sweet Cakes

Extensive listings of soap-tested fragrance oils

www.sweetcakes.com

TKB Trading

Kaila Westerman's outstanding colorant and supply company and source for Gel Tones

www.tkbtrading.com

Wholesale Supplies Plus

Wide range of soapmaking supplies, including airless pumps and foamer bottles

www.wholesalesuppliesplus.com

SMALL BUSINESS SOAPMAKERS

Annabella and Company Creativity Collective

www.annabellaandcompany.com

Celestial Body Natural Arts

www.celestialbody.com

Moon Garden

www.moongarden.us

Woodspirits Ltd., Inc.

www.woodspirits.com

FURTHER READING

Browning, Marie. *Melt & Pour Soapmaking* (New York, NY: Sterling Publications, 2002).

Cavitch, Susan Miller. *The Natural Soap Book* (Pownal, VT: Storey Publishing, 1995).

Cavitch, Susan Miller. *The Soapmaker's Companion* (Pownal, VT: Storey Publishing, 1997).

Coss, Melinda. *The Handmade Soap Book* (Pownal, VT: Storey Publishing, 1998).

Failor, Catherine. *Making Cream Soap Bulletin* (Portland, OR: Milky Way Molds, Inc., 2001)

Failor, Catherine. *Making Natural Liquid Soaps* (Pownal, VT: Storey Publishing, 2000).

Failor, Catherine. *Making Transparent Soap* (Pownal, VT: Storey Publishing, 2000).

Lavabre, Marcel F. *Aromatherapy Workbook* (Rochester, NY: Healing Arts Press, 1990).

Lawless, Julia. *The Illustrated Encyclopedia of Essential Oils* (New York, NY: Element Books, Ltd., 1990).

Letcavage, Elizabeth. *Natural Soap Making* (Mechanicsburg, PA: Stackpole Books, 2013).

Maine, Sandy. *Creating an Herbal Bodycare Business* (Pownal, VT: Storey Publishing, 1999).

Maine, Sandy. *The Soap Book* (Loveland, CO: Interweave, 1995).

McDaniel, Robert, and Katherine J. McDaniel. *Soap Maker's Workshop* (Iola, WI: Krause Publications, 2010).

Westerman, C. Kaila. *Melt and Mold Soap Crafting* (Pownal, VT: Storey Publishing, 2000).

White, Gregory Lee. *Making Soap from Scratch* (Seattle, WA: White Willow Books, 2012).

MAKING MOLDS AND CUTTERS

Inventive and generous soapmaker/carpenter Jennifer Patella has created easy-to-follow instructions for making your wooden soap mold. This is a basic 3-pound mold. The beauty of this box is the fact that the parchment paper fits perfectly in the box and the next day, the paper just pulls out of the box and peels off the soap very easily. These boxes can be used to make regular cold-process soap and hot-process soap in a slow cooker.

MATERIALS

- 1" × 4" board
- 1" × 6" board
- Wood glue
- Nails or wood screws

Patella makes her boxes to fit parchment paper, which is exactly 15$\frac{1}{16}$" wide. You can also make a box to fit freezer paper, which is 18" long. (Your soap batches will need to be increased in size to get the final dimension of your finished product the way you want.)

Inside dimensions are 15$\frac{1}{16}$" × 3½". (Please note that a 1" × 4" board is actually ¾" × 3½".)

ASSEMBLY

1. Cut 3 pieces from the 1" × 4" board, each 15$\frac{1}{16}$" long (one lid and two sides).
2. Cut 2 pieces from the 1" × 4" board: 5$\frac{1}{8}$" long (these will be the two ends).
3. Cut 1 piece from the 1" × 6" board: 16$\frac{9}{16}$" long. (This will be the base; it will be the length of the sides plus the width of the end pieces.) You can make the base longer and have a lip all the way around.

4. Lid and handle: Cut a small piece from whatever is left over from the 1" × 4" board for the handle on the lid. If you prefer, you can purchase a wooden dresser pull or brass handle instead. Just make sure you don't let the nail or screw be in contact with the soap in the box.

5. Assemble the box with wood glue and nails or wood screws.

CUTTERS

If you make soap in big blocks, you may find cutting with a knife, dough scraper, or cheese wire frustrating. You can make very inexpensive and excellent soap cutters using two wooden miter boxes, two guitar strings, four screws, and two cup hooks. You may find these are the only cutters you ever need.

Screw one screw into one side of the miter box, about one-third of the way along the length. Screw another one on the other side at the same place. Screw in the cup hook about ½" away from the screw. Screw the cup hook all the way in, then back it out so that just a few threads are in the wood.

Cut a length of medium-gauge guitar string long enough to wrap around one screw. Go over the sides of the miter box; go around the other screw and wrap onto the cup hook. Leave a little extra on the ends. Make a loop at one end, twisting the wire to make sure it is fast. Loop that around the solo screw. Tightly pass the wire over the top of the miter box, around the other screw, and around the cup hook.

Holding the wire tight, twist the cup hook so it starts to go into the wood, taking up and tightening the wire. Since there aren't a lot of turns on the screw of the cup hook, be sure the wire is quite tight before you start to turn it. Twist until you get a somewhat musical note from the wire.

Repeat with the other miter box, except this time pass the wire through one of the cuts for holding the saw. Run your blocks of soap through the "big" cut first, then through the smaller cut to make bars. Clean off the cutters between uses.

INDEX

Note: Page numbers in *italics* indicate recipes and projects.